Lumbee Indian Girl: Battered but not Shattered

Loretta Hunt Freeman

Copyright © 2011 by Loretta Hunt Freeman

Lumbee Indian Girl: Battered But Not Shattered
by Loretta Hunt Freeman

Printed in the United States of America

ISBN 9781613795231

All rights reserved solely by the author. The author guarantees all contents are original and do not infringe upon the legal rights of any other person or work. No part of this book may be reproduced in any form without the permission of the author. The views expressed in this book are not necessarily those of the publisher.

Unless otherwise indicated, Bible quotations are taken from The Holy Bible, New International Version®. NIV®. Copyright © 1973, 1978, 1984 by International Bible Society®. Used by permission.

Scripture quotations marked KJV are taken from The King James Version.

Scripture quotations marked NKJV™ are taken from The New King James Version®. Copyright © 1982 by Thomas Nelson, Inc. Used by permission. All rights reserved.

Scripture quotations marked NLT are taken from The Holy Bible, New Living Translation. Copyright © 1996. Used by permission of Tyndale House Publishers, Inc., Wheaton, Illinois 60189. All rights reserved.

Scripture quotations marked ESV are taken from the Holy Bible, English Standard Version, Copyright © 2001 by Crossway Bibles, a division of Good News Publishers. Used by permission. All rights reserved.

Scripture quotations marked CEV are taken from The Contemporary English Version®. Copyright © 1995 by American Bible Society. All right reserved.

Edited by Chloe Cummings and Mary Herring

www.xulonpress.com

CONTENTS

Dedications		vii
Acknowledgement		ix
Chapter 1	Childhood Miracles	11
Chapter 2	Shifting and Moving	18
Chapter 3	Family Changes	23
Chapter 4	Life's Detour	30
Chapter 5	Lost Again	35
Chapter 6	Stranger than Strange	38
Chapter 7	Asleep while the Wolf Prowls	44
Chapter 8	The Day of the Smashed Windshield	49
Chapter 9	Maryland: Home of the Firsts	53
Chapter 10	Married Life: The War of the Hunts	56
Chapter 11	Spiraling Downward	59
Chapter 12	Can't Fake the Real Thing	63
Chapter 13	Tie the Knot and Break the Chain	67
Chapter 14	Healing and Wholeness	74
Epilogue		79

Dedications

This book is dedicated to my husband, Carson Samuel Freeman and daughter, Juanita Chavis. May you both continue walking daily with God while allowing Him to guide you. May you always continue growing in your Faith. This book is also dedicated to the memory of my parents, Verdell and Rena Lee Hunt.

Acknowledgements

I give all the praise, glory, and honor, to my Father God and Savior Jesus Christ and to the Holy Spirit who inspired me to begin writing this book. Without God, this book would not have been possible.

Secondly, I want to express my profound gratitude to my husband, Sam Freeman. I wish to thank Sam for his patience, his forbearance, his encouragement, and support throughout the entire process of writing this book.

I would like to acknowledge my precious parents, Verdell Hunt and Rena Lee Hunt, who are deserving of my honor and gratitude, though both are now deceased.

Special thanks to my beautiful sister Ruby Lee and husband Kevin Lee who have always been there for me, whenever I needed them. Special thanks are also extended to my sister Sylvia Lee Jones, who is also my best friend. Thanks to their family members as well.

I thank my brother Wendell Hunt and his wife, Brenda Hunt who encouraged me along the way. I would also like to acknowledge my brothers Verdell and Wade who are both deceased.

I am grateful for my beloved daughter Juanita Chavis, whom God has truly blessed us with. I am thankful for our very wonderful and special grandchildren, Chaplin David Smith and his lovely wife Mary Beth Smith. I also appreciate Ricky Jr., Carlie Hugh Chavis, Tierra and Darrin Collins, and my very own precious name sake Taylor Loretta Josephine Chavis, and all my nieces and nephews.

I would like to acknowledge Pastors Jessie and Roosevelt Singleton, who continue to lift me up in prayer.

I would like to thank all those who prayed for me. Your prayers helped me bring this book to life.

I'd like to also like to recognize the great expression of love that was extended to me by the Lumbee Indian community in North Carolina. I am blessed to be a part of such a community with a heritage rich in traditions, customs, and values that gave me a strong sense of belonging.

I especially would like to acknowledge my friend, Dr. Chloe Cummings who is the author of <u>What Would Jesus Do about Domestic Violence and Abuse towards Christian Women?</u> She is the founder of Back to the Bible Counseling Center in Essex, MD. I appreciate her faithfulness, her encouragement, and the sacrificial time spent working with me on this book.

To all my readers: This book would have little purpose without you. Thanks for your support. I've prayed for each and every one of you.

Chapter 1

Childhood Miracles

~~~?~~~

No single inventor can claim that they invented the hula-hoop, but I am sure that I perfected how it is used. When I was a child, I would step into that yellow circle of joy and hoist it up to my waist. I'd toss that hoop to the right and fling my hips to meet it. I'd shift my hips to the back, and then to right, and then I'd thrust them forward - all the time meeting with the perfect symmetrical shape of that hula-hoop. I'd twist my hips like Elvis and my dance would begin. There wasn't a part of my little body that didn't feel the rhythm of that hula-hoop. I could swing it on my legs, on my arms, and around my neck. My body would gyrate like a top gone wild; I could spin that hula-hoop any which way but loose.

Time would lose track of me and I would lose track of everything else - but my beloved hula-hoop. So one day, when my perfect streak of swinging my hoop over my arm failed, and my hoop flung through the air about 12 feet away and rolled like it had a mind of its own, I had no choice but to run after it. Never mind that it had rolled onto the only major highway that ran through Lumberton, North Carolina in 1958, Highway 301. That highway was just a stone's throw from my front yard.

What happened next could only be recounted by those who were conscious to witness the impact of my little four year old body with a car going no less than 50 mph. I was thrown about 13 feet in the air! I landed in on-coming traffic on that busy highway. Amid the chaos and the screams of onlookers, I slowly became aware of my parents standing over my bloody body.

"Loretta!" "Loretta!" Ma screamed. "Jesus!" "Jesus!" She cried out. Through a fog of haziness, I could see her face which was contorted and fallen from the grunting sounds that were coming from her wailing throat. "Jesus! Loretta! Jesus! Loretta!" She would call both names intermittently like a prayer ascending to heaven and back in rapid succession. Heaven must have answered her back because she changed from a pitiful beggar to an empowered mama with attitude. She began to command my body to live like she was given authority from God Himself. "The word of God states in Psalm 118:17 that she shall not die, but live and declare the works of God!" My mother barked orders like she was a general in somebody's army. My father, now alongside her, had joined the ranks of a heavenly military platoon and raised his voice in unison with hers. "You shall live, in Jesus Name!" they both declared.

It seemed like eternity to me, but within minutes, I was lying in the back of an ambulance heading for Lumberton General Hospital. At the hospital, there was a hub of excitement. Everyone was inquiring about my condition. There was so much blood that it had some people wondering how many bones I may have broken or if I would ever walk again. Some even wondered whether I would live.

Imagine everybody's surprise when, before the day's end, I left the hospital with my parents, walking beside them without one broken bone in my body. I was covered in open wounds that bleed out like oil from a carburetor, but bandages kept the leaks at bay. Apart from my new fashion statement of gauze and tape, I was otherwise unharmed.

My parents admitted to being just as surprised as everyone else at the hospital, but my mom said that she knew God heard her prayers. She credited this miracle to the boldness God gave her to speak the words from the scriptures over me as I laid practically lifeless in the middle of the highway. I was almost destroyed. My body was battered but it was not shattered. That was the beginning of a considerable amount of remarkable and amazing miracles in my life.

≈

My mom and dad grew up with godly parents who both pastored Lumbee churches. One church called Reedy Branch Baptist is still in existence today. They were no strangers to the things of God. They might not have walked the walked, but when in a clutch, they knew how to reach God. My parents, who had good examples to follow, tried their best to give us a childhood which had some resemblance of a good family life.

I remember times when Ma and Daddy would take the whole family downtown to Tom's Café on Fourth Street. My oldest sister Ruby Lee would always get "a hamburger all the way" or what normal people would call a hamburger with everything on it. Sylvia Lee was my next oldest sister and she was a hot dog girl. Wade Godwin was the sibling next in line and he would order anything Ruby Lee ordered. Wendell would order anything that had BBQ sauce on it. I was the next sibling followed by my baby brother Verdell Jr. and being originals, we would order the exact same thing as Ruby and Wade, a hamburger all the way.

After our meal, we would all go to the grocery store to buy our perishables, and then it was on to my favorite store, a local "five and dime" called Ben Franklin. Ben Franklin was always the cherry on top of my day because, as well as being a small haven for many types of toys, Ben Franklin sold hula-hoops.

My family lived in a community of mostly Lumbee Indians like us. Coming into our yard was a pleasure. The first thing that greeted me was the large Oak tree which held the tree house that Daddy built for us children. He nailed wide pieces of boards on the trunk which escalated up to the top of the tree. Many times, I would secure my arms and legs onto those boards and climb up to greet my tree house before I would even step onto the porch of our home. That Oak tree was only rivaled by the large Chinaberry tree that loomed in our backyard like a giant security guard whose only job was to shade the back porch which Daddy also built.

After visiting my tree house, I'd scale down the trunk, sprint across the big yard, and run up the three steps onto that large front porch. Often times, I'd ignore the glorious spray of rose bushes which framed the porch from one end to the other, but sometimes, I'd stop to pick a petal off of one and press it between my lips. It would inevitably end up in my mouth where I'd swallow it like it was rose candy.

Opening the front door, I'd enter a small foyer and the first place I'd head for would be the kitchen. The kitchen was large enough to hold an oversized wooden table which could comfortably seat all eight of us right in the center of the kitchen. Being so close to Ma's stove made her cooking all the sweeter.

I would rarely glance at the room to the right of the foyer because it was the sitting room and we kids were not allowed to play in there. Though it was directly across from the kitchen, that special room was very important. Entering that room was like entering my family's own history museum. Hanging on the wall were brown-tinged pictures of two sets of grandparents from both sides. Their portraits were set in large oval frames with glass that was more curved than flat. In the center of my grandparents' portraits was one large picture of my parents. They were standing close and smiling so widely that just looking at their picture gave me a warm happy feeling inside. Pictures of each of us children taken at various stages of our lives were on two of the other walls in the room. One could walk from one picture to the other and make a full circuit around the room. The stately hunter green sofa and the four wing chairs which were placed strategically around the room awaited the visitors and guests that would sometimes drop by.

The most used room in our house outside of the kitchen was the living room. This large room was the place where all eight member of our family would gather together in the evening on any given day of the week. Ma would sit in the rose patterned love seat and read The Grit, a local tabloid newspaper. Dad would be sprawled out on the sofa letting the TV watch him snore. The six of us kids would watch the only show which all of us uniformly agreed was the best, Bonanza!

Sometimes, when I wanted to be by myself, I'd simply open the door of the living room and step out onto the enclosed back porch that Daddy had built on to the back of the house.

My other get-away place was my bedroom. The picture of a bright red rooster guarding a barn was the first thing I saw when I opened my eyes in the mornings. I had a large toy chest which didn't get to hold many toys because most of my toys were strewn on the floor and under the bed. Verdell Jr. and I shared the same room so matchbox cars and action figures were intermingled in the mess. The one piece of furniture that was the center-piece to our room was a hefty wooden bunk-bed. That bed was like a jungle gym and safari all in one. It was not uncommon for three or more of us to jump and swing and perform all sorts of contortions on that bed.

One day, Wade and I were in my room playing around. He was jumping up and down like a monkey on the top bunk. I was on the bottom bunk hollering at him for some reason. Suddenly a crash, followed by a blow of pain, struck my head.

My head felt like a hammer had just slammed down on it as if it were a coconut which was smashed into pieces. I reached up my hands to touch my head and blood oozed through my fingers. It began running down my arms. Within seconds my clothes was soaked. When I saw the blood I started to scream!

Wade, hanging over the rail of the bunk bed above me, began yelling with a death scream for my mother. "Ma! Ma!" He looked so frightened and I knew from the terror that I saw in my older brother's face that things were worse than my mind could imagine.

The blood had now run down my neck and all over my shirt. Mindlessly, I began to scream at the top of my lungs. The pain rushed throughout my body. My head throbbed terribly. It felt as if a 3-inch nail had been stuck in it. In fact, that's exactly what had happened. The nail was driven right into my head! I didn't realize what had happened at that moment, but one of the boards from the top bunk had crashed under Wade's feet and had landed on my head, fully secured and embedded in my skull.

My brother jumped down out of the bed. He was as pale as self-rising flour. He kept screaming over and over like a broken record, "Oh my God! She is dead! Oh my God! She is dead!" Although my mother was there within a couple seconds, it could have been too long because I was losing blood rapidly. I had now collapsed into unconsciousness. Seeing the seriousness of my plight, the blood now everywhere, plus hearing Wade's declaration that I was dead, my mother believed for one horrifying moment that I really was.

I do not remember the drive to Lumberton General Hospital that day nor do I recall arriving there. I was told that the medical staff laid me on a gurney and rolled me to the emergency room. I learned later that the nail in the board went into my skull through the bone and touched my brain. The doctors had no medical explanation as to why I didn't lose all the blood in my body. I remember that I was unable to move my head and I was aware of people walking around. The sound of clanging tools filled the emergency room.

The doctors kept their voices low so I had trouble following what they were saying. I remember thinking that something terrible had happened and I sensed it had happened to me. Even though I could hear the voices, I thought I was dead. One voice said, "There is nothing we can do for her." Another voice said, "She is not going to make it." There were more muffled voices, and more clanging. My head still hurt but in a strange way, and through the clangs and the mixture of sounds, I heard a clear voice, "She won't leave here alive this time." They wheeled me into another room.

My accident had sobered my mother and father back into a place where they would sometimes leave and return to in desperate times like this. They were in a place of brokenness and repentance and calling out to God who was certainly more faithful to them than they were to Him. As they rolled the gurney past my parents, I could hear my mother and father quoting Matthew 27:25. "Then answered all the people and said, His blood be on us, and on our children." This was a scripture that I heard my grandparents say all the time, but this was the first and only time I heard it from my parents' lips. I remembered seeing an incomprehensibly large number of people and thinking that these were angels. I fixed my eyes on one particular lady for a split second and then she shocked me with a loud scream, "This little girl is looking at me! She's awake!" I later understood that I was not the only one that was shocked because I was taken as dead and that woman saved me from going to the morgue.

They took me into a room where the doctor was waiting for me. It seemed strange but the only thing I recall about the doctor was hearing him say, "I don't believe it!" He was shocked. After spending quite a while checking me over, he told my parents that I was seriously hurt but he would do everything that he could. Despite his words, I later learned that he didn't expect me to survive. I passed out again.

≈

God can do in one single night what man would take months or even years to do. I guess if I could have imagined God coming in my hospital room that night, my five year old mind would have imagined something like a Walt Disney fairy creature flying around my bed and sprinkling sparkly pixy dust on top of me. Of course, this would be accompanied by the sound of enchanting tinkling music which testifies to the magical powers which were directed at me. But in truth, God visited me that first night in the hospital. Though I wasn't aware that anything magical had taken place, I woke up the next morning as new as ever. The only sensation I felt was a little lightheadedness.

The doctors were mesmerized by the amazing recovery that had taken place overnight. They could not believe it. They checked me over before admitting that they could not find any medical reason to keep me in the hospital. The word spread throughout the hospital of this miraculous recovery and as Ma wheeled me through the hospital, I felt like I was somebody famous because nurses and doctors would stop us just to talk with me. I could feel this excitement all around me, and when we got outside, nurses and doctors actually applauded as we walked over to our car.

As Ma and I walked to our car, I heard my mother softly say, "Lord, we thank you for protecting our daughter and healing her from the top of her head to the soles of her feet - in the name of Jesus." I couldn't say it then, but I believe that I survived only because of my parents' prayers. I only wished that they had kept themselves in that place where God was there to help them because there were other surprises waiting for my family. However, my mother and father failed to keep in touch with God like they had once done.

Chapter 2

Shifting and Moving

∽∾∾∾∾

S cientists tell us that the surface of the earth is made up of independent sections called plates and these plates have the ability to shift and move. They say that for the most part, we are unaware of any changes happening but sometimes these plates collide with each other and such catastrophes like earthquakes and volcanoes can occur. I think of the summer of 1960 as a time when the different sections that made up *my* life began to shift and move. At first, the shift in the otherwise stable segments of my life was subtle, but later on, challenges caused various parts to collide. In the end, the result was catastrophic.

It all began when our father came home one day with the news that there was no more work in the surrounding area of Robeson County for him. Around dinner time, he hollered out, "Alright guys, everybody come together. I have something to share with all of you." We kids must have sensed something in that otherwise normal call to the kitchen table because Ruby, Wade, Sylvia, Wendell, Verdell Jr. and I got to the big kitchen table all bound together like a six-pack of beer. We didn't want to hear dad holler "Don't let me have to tell you one more time now!"

At the table, there was a somber feeling in the atmosphere and I knew that all this heaviness was coming from my dad. He had this expression on his face that borderlined on sheer desperation. Like a bad house guest, sadness came home with him, and I could see wetness in his eyes. I wanted to reach my arms out to him and give him a hug but I knew that was not the thing to do because there was no way my daddy would ever allow anyone to see him cry. The spoon was clanging against the side of the pots as my mother prepared to put the food on the table, and while the chicken and pastry was being dished onto our plates, dad dished out his own story. "Things don't look so good" he started. "Work has dried up, and we can't maintain things around here." By "work" he meant crop-picking work. My father had worked on farms as a laborer picking various kinds of crops all his life. He kept saying things like "crunch time" and "changes" and using words like "finances", but he didn't grab my attention until I heard "....so we have to move to Florida."

Move to Florida! For me, the mood suddenly shifted from somber to jubilant. An adventurous trip to Florida was about to take place and I was all ears. He continued to talk about a person he knew that lived in Okeechobee, Florida. This person was searching for workers. He said that he was preparing to relocate as soon as possible. I could contain my excitement no longer. I got up and began to jump. My brothers and sisters were chattering excitedly and Dad had to raise his voice to null the excitement. "Now hold up!" he blew out his words like a coach calling a team to quiet down. "You children cannot come to Florida with us."

For a split second, quiet came over the room! He continued, "...not yet anyway." But that didn't soften the blow. He said that he and Ma would have to go ahead and secure this job and then find us a place to live. We will stay behind until they send for us. Devastated! That's how we felt. Sections of my life had just collided and my world crashed right before my eyes. I began to scream and my screams turned into screeches and then bellows of sobs poured out. I begged my daddy and Ma not to leave me behind but their voices just got more serious and determined.

"Quiet down!" dad used his 'I'm-not-playing-with-you' voice and stunned me and my siblings back to attention. He explained to us that we would move to Aunt Arretta's house and live with her for a few months. Our aunt lived in Robeson County and we would be able to go to the same school and minimize further changes in our lives.

My eldest sister Ruby, after hearing that this dramatic change was occurring in our family, decided that she was old enough to move out on her own. My parents didn't oppose her decision to the degree that I thought they would. Maybe guilt has its benefits.

Within a matter of weeks, my parents left for Okeechobee, Florida. Now that Ruby had made her stance for independence, it was my sister Sylvia, my three brothers, and I who showed up at Aunt Arretta's front door. Mom and dad had dropped us off and their goodbyes marked the saddest day of my life up until that point. I thought that though I had survived major head injury and a collision with a car, I would not survive my parents leaving me behind. My hope for life hung on their promise that we would be joining them in Florida once school was out.

≈

My aunt was a single middle-aged Christian woman with a strong religious background. When we arrived at her house, she immediately laid out the house rules for us. She said, "One thing that I don't tolerate is disrespectful children. You mind your manners and we'll be okay." She went on to tell us about her Sunday rules, "And another thing, we leave for Church at 8:00 every Sunday morning. Be ready. In this house, we serve the Lord!" I got the message that staying home on Sundays wasn't an option but I didn't mind because I loved going to Church anyway.

As time continued to move forward, all of us were becoming more and more comfortable living with Aunt Arretta. She would always read and tell Bible stories. She also prayed with us every night. I liked living with someone who had a consistent regiment of godly living patterns. My parents didn't seem to have that personal bond with God on such a consistent basis as my aunt did. Aunt Arretta was really such a meek and humble person, whom we knew loved us, despite her no-nonsense attitude. Over the period of the nine-month school year, our aunt spent unlimited time devoted to taking care of our needs. Just by the way she lived she taught us so much about God. She unwittingly taught us about values and principles and what it meant to be a true Christian. We missed Daddy and Ma, but honestly, outside of our parents, no one could have loved us more.

On the last day of school, the school bell rang indicating the start of summer vacation. Our parents rang to affirm that they would be sending for us. What a splendid phone call that was. We were to take the Greyhound bus to Okeechobee, Florida. I was very excited. My brothers Wade, Wendell, and Verdell Jr., were also bubbling over with excitement, but Sylvia was not saying much of anything. Soon what was inside Sylvia came out; she wanted to continue staying with Aunt Arretta. When she announced her wishes to my parents over the phone, I could tell that they were not happy about it but they knew she would be well cared for and she would also be able to finish out her senior year at the same high school. I would never have imagined that Sylvia's staying was a better deal in many ways than what was waiting for my brothers and me in Florida.

≈

Between the bumps on the road and our excitement to be going back to be with our parents, we could hardly keep our butts in our seats. When the bus finally eased into the bus station, our searching eyes landed squarely on Daddy and Ma. They were equally as anxious to see us. When we got off that Greyhound bus, we were wrapped and smothered in bear hugs and kisses. I don't think all the holidays, Christmas and Thanksgiving included, held as much joy for me as that moment.

Once we acquired our belongings, we got in the car and headed to our new home. We were very eager and excited to see where we were going to live. Surely, with Daddy's success of finding work in Florida, we no doubt had a large and beautiful home waiting for us. I was especially interested in knowing whether Daddy had built us a new tree house. Maybe I'll have my own bedroom and wouldn't have to share with Verdell Jr.

On the drive home, our parents asked how things had been and we jabbered on and on about all that we had done with Aunt Arretta. Before long, the conversation turned to our new home. "Alright guys, don't expect your home to be like the one we had in North

Carolina." Daddy said in some kind of a sing-song voice. "Of course not" I thought. In North Carolina, we lived in a single family house, with a big yard, three bedrooms and plenty of room to play. With Daddy's new job, I could only expect better! I knew that only rich people and tourists lived in the Sunshine State in those days. Dad continued speaking, "a lot of things have changed and we have to make-due with the house we live in now." I was puzzled. *What is he saying?* "When things improve, we can move to a better home, but for now, everybody has to pull together to make ends meet." He was talking a little faster now. "...that means all of you have to go to work with us this summer." *"Work!?"* What was he really saying to us? Before I could wrap my mind around what my father was saying, he continued more crazy talk.

"We've got to work a lot now. We have to work seven days a week so me and your mother can't go to Church like we used to." Put the brakes on! Not go to Church!? I totally missed the child-labor part of my dad's declaration. All that was repeating itself in my mind was "No church." I was so shocked that I blurted out, "No church! How can that be? We always go to church!" I could not understand how it was possible that we would not be going to church anymore. We were raised up in church. My parent's lives had always revolved around religious activities. Now it seemed that they were leaving God behind.

I felt a pang of longing for Aunt Arretta's. Even in my young life, I had an un-explainable fear that my parents' decision to leave the Church and God behind was a sign that our future was getting ready to take a nose-dive!

Chapter 3

Family Changes

We pulled up in front of a building and parked. My parents said, "OK guys, you are home!" I looked and I didn't see a house. I asked, "Where is the house?" My father told us that this *was* our house. I said, "This is not a house; this is a barn - a place where animals live. I want to know where our house is Daddy?" My father's voice turned serious and with a deep tone he affirmed, "This *is* your home." Our "home" was really a labor camp site. Nowadays, we may refer to such a place as a refugee camp. It was one long building which looked similar to railroad boxcars without the connection in between. In each "box" lived a worker family regardless of how many members each family had. A front door was the only way in and out of each house and there were no windows.

We got out of the car and walked into the "house". I could not believe my eyes! We were standing in a single room that was approximately 17 X 20 feet. It was sweltering inside because there was no ventilation. Dad propped the door open so those giant Floridian beetle bugs could fly in along with the fresh air. My brother asked, "Where are the beds? Where do we sleep?" My father motioned downwards and said, "On the floor." As it turned out, the floor not only served as our beds but also as our dining table, our sofa, our countertop, and anything else we wanted it to be. The only "furniture" in the house was a hot plate and several cardboard boxes that acted as shelves for plates and other things.

During our first dining experience on our rustic floor, my father said he wanted to take this time while we were eating to explain more about the circumstances that had changed our lives. He began his conversation by telling us that the move to Florida had not turned out as he had hoped. He said that the living conditions were very poor and we did not have enough money to find a better house right away. We were together and that is what matters. He continued, "Children, we just have to make-do with what we have right now. Just give it time; we will pull together and save our money." He reached over and gave Wade a playful slap on the back. "Things are looking up already", he said with a smile. He was referring to the fact that we children were there to work and we would be bringing more money into our home. I listened attentively so that I too, could make sense of our new situation.

He then spent some time explaining the kind of work that we would be doing. We were going to work in the vegetable fields, starting at 7:00am and ending at 4:00pm. We were going to be working along with thirty or forty other people, most of whom were Lumbee Indians like us. Everyone would be riding on the bus to and from the fields. At the end of each work day, the contractor would give the bus driver our money, and on the return trip home on the bus, the driver would give each person $7.00. That was one day's pay. He explained that it was beneficial for my siblings and me to work with him because we would *each* get $7.00, and that would mean more money for our family.

This made sense to us in our minds but confusion remained in our hearts. I felt somewhat betrayed by my parents and I also felt jealous of my friends who were doing fun summer activities. Many of my school friends were attending summer camp. Some went to Camp Jude, some went to the YMCA, others went to Grace Camp, but my brothers and I were going to *labor* camp.

The fun started within days of our arrival. All the families in the camp loaded up on the bus at 5:00am because we would travel to different fields at various locations. If you picture the image of slaves in a cotton field with their backs bent and heads bowed over cotton plants, you would get an accurate picture of us, but instead of cotton, we would mostly pick tomatoes (which grew on vines that ran along the ground). The mechanics of our bodies bending low and arms going back and forth to pick tomatoes, green peppers, or whatever the "pick of the day" was, and putting the crop into the baskets or foot-tubs, could rival any factory equipment. When our tubs or baskets were full, we would walk to where the big bin of water was and dumped what we picked in it. We would then return to start the process again. We kids were assembly line parts that had to produce a respectable amount of work. If we were getting adult wages, we had better produce adult work! By the end of a burning hot day, our bus would carry adults and little kids who were utterly exhausted. Though we often started our trip off being rambunctious, we would invariably fall asleep before we got back to our boxcar homes.

That summer was one which I hated but it set the pattern of many more summers to come. I was glad to get back in school. My brothers and I adjusted to the change of our new school well, but it was the changes in our home that mainly concerned me.

≈

At home, our world was turning upside down. Due to our seven-day work-week, my parents had long since stopped going to church. Other things replaced our former family times of Bible reading and loving conversations. Instead of the harmony we once had, our parents spent much of our family time now shouting and screaming at each other. They would carry on like that for days. We had never heard our parents argue before. Now, they were arguing every other day. Afterwards, they would become silent towards each other for long periods of time. Subsequently, the whole house was filled with a deep and disturbing quiet. Often, silence would be interrupted by blasts of ferocious arguments which gradually became longer and more frequent. Soon, hearing mom scream, "I don't have to put up with this!" and then slamming the door behind her, became a regular occurrence. I thought that starting arguments with dad and leaving the scene became her way of getting out of the oppressive atmosphere that was our home.

One day, my father sat us down following a major dispute after which Ma had made her grand exit. "Your mother's been drinking" he said. "She started last year when you all were at Arretta's." His voice was like a flat-line on a heart monitor machine pronouncing somebody dead. "She won't listen to me. I keep begging her to stop for all your sakes but she's like…" He paused, "…living at the bar these days." He started showing a lot more emotion which looked more like regret, "I hate to tell you all this really, but I can't keep it a secret any longer."

As time passed, we noticed that there would be days when my mother would not go to work because she did not come home the night before. She would disappear for days on top of days. This went on even as school started in the fall and remained for the rest of the school year.

My brothers and I were becoming accustomed to Ma slipping into her regular drink joint, a place called Ma Brown's. Often times, she would not go to work with us because she was there. There were also times when we had to go to the bar and plead with her to come home with us. It was like dragging a thirsty animal from his watering hole.

We didn't understand what was happening to our mother and why the drinking had control of her life. We did not know how she had gotten to that point in life, nor did we know how long she would stay that way. It took a trip back to North Carolina the following summer to give us an answer.

≈

Around the Fourth of July, my parents decided that we would go to visit my Aunt Arretta. While there, we planned on bringing my sister Sylvia, back home with us. As it turned out, Sylvia didn't join us on the return trip. She continued living with Aunt Arretta. On the way to North Carolina, I stared remembering what it was like when I was living with my aunt. I felt like a traitor for wishing that my parents' home was more like Aunt Arretta's because I was so grateful to be with them, yet I could not squelch the feelings of wanting to live where God obviously hung out.

Once we arrived at my aunt's house, there was much excitement. It was great to see my sister Sylvia again. During our time with Aunt Arretta and our sister, we visited many friends, cousins, and other relatives. It was good to be back in an environment that we were familiar with - one with most of my Lumbee Indian relatives. Lumbee Indians have strong family values and believe that marriages are forever. They also believe that families should have strong bonds so it was really comforting to be around them. I felt good to be in such a communal family though I didn't realize at the time that my own was about to be torn apart.

≈

My father remembered my aunt's rules in reference to staying at her house; mainly that everyone had to go to church on Sundays. When Sunday came, we did go to church with my aunt and sister. I was so excited to be back in church because we had not gone since we had left for Florida. I was hoping that my parents would realize how much we as a family, needed God. I felt that if we would just go to church and go back to God, then our family would be well again. As things progressed, I realized that I was the only one with that thought.

After church, we returned to my aunt's house to eat dinner and to spend some quality time as a family. We had been there five days already when my father said that we would leave for Florida on Wednesday which was three days away. After we finished dinner, my mother decided to take a walk. I asked if I could go walking with her but she insisted that I stay behind. She continued to walk on by herself. That stroll turned into my mother becoming a missing person.

By nightfall, Ma had not returned from her walk. We began to worry, and then worry turned to panic. My brothers and I went with my father and we began searching for her throughout the night. My brothers and I were in our own world of terror. Words were not spoken except to offer aloud ideas of places where we thought she might be. Silence blanketed our search and intensified with the darkness as our fears increased. The silence would only be broken by our frantic yells as we hollered out in unison "Ma! Ma!" We searched for hours and hours until the dawn came. She was nowhere to be found.

My brothers and I didn't want to stop searching but Daddy insisted that we go back to the house. I was so devastated that we could not find my mother. Our bodies were tired. We tried to sleep but we couldn't. After about two hours of rest, we began our pursuit again. We spent the entire day looking for her but we had no luck. When the sun went down, we stopped looking for my mother. My dad looked discouraged and defeated. I trusted that he knew how to solve any problem, but as I looked at him, any thread of hope which I had slipped into oblivion.

My father said that if Ma was not back by the next day, she would be left behind in North Carolina. Those were the cruelest words I've ever heard my dad speak. I don't know why we didn't call the police to report her missing. Looking back, I realized that my father may have thought that she was not in any mortal danger.

When we arose the following morning, my mother had still not returned. We began to pack our clothes into our suitcases. I kept expecting my mother to barge through the door of my aunt's house at any moment. I could not image leaving her behind. I kept glancing at the front door believing that she would surprise us and return in time to go back to Florida with us. After we finished packing, my father asked if we were ready to hit the road. We each said yes, but in our hearts we were not ready to go at all…not without our mother! I wondered how my dad could be so cruel as to leave Ma behind.

As we said our farewells and got into the car for Florida, my siblings and I continued to look back, each of us praying that Ma would come around the corner before the car could pull out of sight. But that did not happen. As we drove off, I began to cry and sob like I never had before. My heart was pounding so hard I felt like it was going to burst wide open. It was breaking! I thought I was going to die. I had never felt such pain up until that point, and fear was gripping and consuming me. Even the nail that was embedded in my skull when I was five did not cause this level of pain. I could not think of anything else but the thought of losing my mother forever.

I was so consumed with fear that it caused sweat to pop from my temples. Fear turned into rage and my body began to tremble all over. The weight of losing my mother was too much to bear and my fury turned towards my dad for leaving her behind. I could not believe that my father would not wait until she returned or at least make sure that she was alright and that no harm had come to her. I needed my mother!

I had to let my feelings out and I began jumping up and down in the back seat of the car and yelling at my father. "I can't believe you left Ma!" I screamed. "Why didn't you wait? Why did you leave her?" I began to demand that he turn the car around and go back to look for my mother again. "You wouldn't leave a *dog* like that. How would you like it if we left *you!*?" I challenged. "I hate you! I hate you! I hate you!" These words erupted from me like rounds from a gun and I emptied the barrel of bullets into him. I soon figured out that my dad was not going to turn the car around so my demands turned into pleas, and I began to beg my father to turn around and go back to look for Ma one more time. "Daddy, please! Daddy, please! Let's go back, please!"

Suddenly, my father pulled the car off to the side of the road. He had lost all patience with me. "Shut up!" He yelled. "If you don't shut up, I'll take this belt off and tear your butt up!" That motivated me, so I kindly sat back down on the seat and sobbed quietly.

Chapter 4

Life's Detours

As we continued on our journey back to Florida, my father began to tell us things regarding our mother which we had not known before. My outburst had compelled him to share things which he had kept locked inside for many years. He began "Your mother's not lost, and your mother is not dead. Your Mother is having some trouble in her mind." All I heard was that Ma's not dead. There was no greater gift he could have given us than those precious words. I didn't know how much worry I was carrying until I partially collapsed against Verdell Jr. from relief. Dad started to tell us things about our mother that if I didn't know better, I would say that he was making them up.

$\approx$

Daddy began his story. "Back when Sylvia was born, your mother had a real hard time. Truth be known, she had a nervous breakdown. Gosh, I didn't know what to do. One minute, she'd be fine and the next minute, she'd be cussing me out something major. She'd just start hitting on me for no reason and going all crazy. I don't think there's one thing Rena Lee didn't accuse me of." Daddy was using Ma's name like he was talking to himself and not us.

"She'd say I was lying all the time or I was leaving the house to see other women. Good Lord, I had enough with just one!" He quipped. Maybe he was trying to lighten up things for us. It didn't work. My brothers and I were silent. It was like hearing a story from a book, except this was about our Ma. "I had to always watch out for her because sometimes she'd leave the house and go wandering around the neighborhood in her nightie. She would talk about wanting to die all the time. One time, she tried to jump into the well out back. It's a good thing it wasn't totally dark outside yet because if it had been, I wouldn't have seen her and run to catch her before she jumped...well..." His voice trailed off before gathering more fuel to continue.

"Rena Lee! What are you doing?" I hollered at her. "I grabbed her around the waist right before the bottom half of her body followed where the upper half was going. Your Ma was fighting me off like I was the one doing her harm. She screamed, 'Leave me alone Verdell, you don't care about me!' It was like wrestling an alligator. Finally, I just had to pick her up underneath her butt, throw her over my shoulder and carry her inside. She was so strong for a little woman who didn't weigh even 110 pounds soaking wet. Your Ma called me all sorts of names but my own, because I intercepted her from doing the one thing which she believed would end her pain."

Dad continued on. He told us that Ma's suicide attempt was his wakeup call, and the next day he admitted her into Chapel Hill Hospital in Raleigh-Durham, North Carolina. She wasn't there long before the hospital diagnosed her as a crazy Indian and transferred her to the wing reserved for the crazy people, the mental ward.

That's when things went from bad to worse. The horrors which my mother experienced were never told, not even from her own lips, but her right arm, shattered from the elbow to the wrist, told its own story. She lost 50 pounds in the next six months, and for a 4'11" woman who had weighed only 110 pounds, that was nothing short of horrifying. Dad said that every two weeks he would visit Ma and she would beg him, "Please Verdell, take me outta here, pleeeeze!"

My dad confessed that he refused to take her out simply because, in part, he didn't understand what she was going through. Also, his hope for help was anchored too deeply in the hospital's promise that she would get better. He saw her getting worse but he consoled himself with the thought that things often times get worse before they get better.

The day when things got better came. Ma's doctor changed her medication. She began to improve over a short period of time. After that, Daddy said that he took Ma home from the hospital a lot thinner woman with a right arm that stayed in a noticeable "L" position for the rest of her life.

In the back seat of the car, we kids listened to our father tell this story like it was a drama on the radio and we didn't want him to turn the dial. "Tell us more Daddy." we were screaming inside, and as if reading our thoughts, he continued. "Your mother came home with a special medication they gave her. Things looked good for a while but, after a couple of days, I found her staggering around the house like she just had a fifth of Vodka. Your mother never drank! Not then anyways. She would literally fall over chairs and trip over her feet. I had to pick her up off of the floor many times. She was slurring and her eyes were glazy." Daddy was talking like he was really there now. "I put two and two together and took a good look at the medication the hospital had given your ma. The pills that she took at the hospital were red; the ones she had at home were red. Also, the bottle was almost empty." Daddy's audience in the back seat was mesmerized.

Daddy continued. He told us that he called the hospital and after checking Ma's medical records, they confirmed that she was given the wrong medication. Also, Ma had taken most of the 30-day supply of pills in 3 days. The bottle was empty before the end of the day and Daddy said that he refused to fill the new prescription, even if it was the properly prescribed one. By now, Ma's body was accustomed to being high and intoxicated from taking prescription medications due to her lengthy stay in the mental hospital and also by her near-overdose on those little red pills.

Since daddy had refused to help Ma get her legal narcotics, she went to the store herself and bought some Spirits of Ammonia. Spirits of Ammonia is an over-the-counter medicine traditionally used as smelling salts to energize people who faint. Nevertheless, it was legal and accessible. People would make ammonia water to cool the body down on hot days, and that would involve mixing

¾ of a 2 oz. bottle of Spirits of Ammonia to 1 gallon of water and ice. Ma would not mix it. She would drink a 2 oz. vial straight, and then pass-out for two whole days. Her constitution was like that of a horse because, as an addict, she subjected her body to this "treatment" for the next two years and yet, she lived to have four more children.

Thank God that with Daddy's help, and also over a period of time, she weaned herself off these "medicines" and went on to have healthy children. Things were getting back to normal for Rena Lee and Verdell Sr. They began to focus on having a stable lifestyle which included going back into a life of church-going and practicing their faith. But, that monkey of addiction as my mother's answer to dealing with life's pressure, still haunted her, and it would return years later to take her away forever.

≈

As my dad finished relating our mother's story to us, things were clicking in my mind like puzzle parts being snapped into place. I could see that he was tired after years of fighting this battle, and now he had given up the fight and was returning now without his wife. Wade, Wendell, Verdell Jr. and I were returning home without our mother. I felt like Daddy had not only flung open a secret door into Ma's past life but he had given us a tour which we would never forget. Now "armed" with some answers to why Ma drank like she did and why she would fight so hard to get to her alcohol, even at the expense of leaving her family, my pain began to ease up somewhat.

That day, I formed some opinions about life which I never consciously had before. First, Lumbee Indians get sick in the mind and sick in the heart just like anyone else. Second, *my* family was not exempt from bad things which break up families. Third, I had the most striking realization that the road of life has detours; and sometimes we can get lost and do not know how to get back on the right path. My mother was set on a path of alcoholism by a misdiagnosis and wrong prescriptions, and though she got back on the straight and narrow for a while, she detoured to a place that took her away from us.

As I saw it, life was similar to that move to Florida. We may start off with glorious plans and intentions, but there can be unexpected detours on our journey and the road can take us to places where we never intended to go. We can end up being left bereft of hope; just like I was now…driving back home to Okeechokee without my mother.

Chapter 5

Lost Again

As time went on, things at home began to return to normal. We had pretty much resigned to thinking that Ma was not coming back. We kids went back to working in the vegetable fields to help bring some money into our home. Summer turned into fall and we started a new school year. Over that time, I could see that our dad was changing. His bright countenance was becoming tarnished and he seemed to be uneasy about something. It could be that he had a notion of what was about to take place, but we were taken totally off guard.

One day, we got off the bus after a long day at work, and walking to our house, we saw our mom standing in front of our door. When I saw her standing there, it was like seeing an angel from Heaven. She had cleaned up marvelously. She looked so pretty and refreshed to me. I was very happy to see her. I quickly ran up the path to her and grabbed her by her waist. "Ma, I missed you, I missed you so much." I kept telling her over and over how much I missed her and how much I loved her. She lifted my small body up into her arms and gave me the sweetest hug. I didn't want her to let me go. I wanted to feel that love forever. Wade, Wendell, and Verdell Jr. had run along with me and were vying for their turn to get in on the love fest.

Daddy walked right past our hoopla, through the door and closed it behind him. He did not look happy at all. After a few more minutes with us, Ma knocked on the door. My father opened it with constraint. Sheepishly she said, "Hi Verdell. Can I talk with you for a minute?" Daddy turned away and walked further into the house. Ma followed him, closing the door behind her.

Standing outside, we were so excited that we could hardly breathe. We didn't even talk because we were anxious to hear what was going on in the house. Each one was jockeying for a good spot on the door to press an ear against it. Our future was dependent on the outcome of what was going on in the little box house. Hope was building up in my heart as I imagined that my parents would reconcile and we would go on as a real family again.

We didn't expect to be blasted by my mom's words which sailed through the cracks in the front door several minutes later. "I hate you!" she flared. "I hate you for doing this to me." An argument was in full swing, but it seemed that Ma was the only one yelling. She was telling dad that he was no good and that he was going to suffer for doing this (whatever 'this' was) to her. Soon, we heard dad flare back at her. "I'm sick and tired of you leaving and coming back. I'm sick of your drama!" He was saying more things but we were only getting bits and pieces of what was a very heated argument.

Suddenly, Daddy flung open the front door and ordered Ma out of his house, "Don't let the door hit you in the back!" Ma was now beet red with tears bursting out of her face from being so angry. "I'll find me another man; just you wait and see. I'll fix you!" she threatened. She turned and ran from the house faster than I'd ever seen her run before. As far as I was concerned, she was running out of my life and leaving me behind... again.

I began to cry and wail, not quite understanding what had transpired behind those closed doors. She was running away so fast. I began screaming, "Ma wait! Please wait! Ma, please don't go!" She continued to run and I could not catch up to her. Why wouldn't she stop? Didn't she love us? I was screaming with everything I had inside me but she just kept running like her skirt was on fire. She was now out of my sight and I was left heaving in the middle of the sidewalk. My brother Wendell came and got me. We were both crying uncontrollably. The hurt I felt was twisting my entire insides into knots. Then Wendell said something to me which ministered to my heart, "Sis, it's going to be OK. God will help us make it through." Coming from my thirteen year old brother, one who was three years my senior, those words meant more to me than anything else.

Once back inside, my father gave us a speech about loving Ma and praying for Ma. Even though I don't remember all he said, I knew he was trying to comfort us, but I didn't feel any better. He said that Ma was back and living in Florida and we shouldn't be surprised if we happen to see her again.

The next time we saw my mother, she was coming out of Ma Brown's, her old haunt. She was drunk like she was now caretaker to bottles of Schlitz beer rather than caretaker of her children. In her intoxicated state she did remember that she was not with us anymore. She slobbered and slurred many apologies to us. Ma admitted that she needed some help with her drinking problem and said that she would get help one day. She also said that she wanted us to always know that she loved us no matter what. Her parting words were, "I'll see you soon." It was several days since she had run away from our house and my brothers and I could not help but cry all over again.

≈

Little did we realize that "soon" would be the very next day! To everyone's surprise, especially my dad's, Ma was on the work bus headed to the vegetable field to work with us. Dad might not have been pleased but I really enjoyed my mother being in the vegetable field with us. I felt like God was answering my prayers. I had my mother near me. She was sober and I could talk to her all day. My brothers and I would work beside her and we would maneuver our pickings so that we would be as close to her as possible.

Over the next several months, my mother began to change, and much for the better. She started looking really good. She had quit drinking again. She also found herself a boyfriend! She looked like she was beginning to enjoy herself because she didn't look wore down anymore. I felt proud of her because she had stopped drinking and everyone could see that things were going well for her. Everyone, except for my dad!

Chapter 6

Stranger than Strange

We never know how one person's choice impacts another, but sometimes the outcome can be unpredictable and downright ugly. My father would not talk to us anymore about our mother. I think it was because he could see that she had moved on with her life and in a sense had abandoned him as a wife. When he saw her with a man for the first time, he was noticeably shocked. Daddy's face was not built to hide feelings. Anguish and jealously showed all over him. Before long, the torment he felt on the inside began to manifest itself on the outside.

The first thing to slip was his appearance. He began to look run down. His demeanor fell. He dressed sloppily, and things only got worse. Daddy started spending more and more time by himself and less time paying attention to us. We also began to notice that he would have the smell of alcohol on him. We didn't question him right away about the smell because he was also becoming increasingly irritable and grumpy.

It was about that time that things seemed to steam-roll, with one unpredictable change right after another. First of all, the season for working in the vegetable fields in Florida had ended. This meant that we would have to relocate again to another state, along with the other migrant workers. When I see movies of the old American West which show Indian tribes packing up their tepees and other belongings to follow the trail of the buffalo, I think of those childhood days of migration, except what provided food on the table and clothes on our backs were farmlands instead of buffalo. Of course, that meant that we would have to adjust to a new school, meet new friends, and work in the fields when school was out. I didn't like the idea of working but I did like the chance to travel, or so I thought.

All the migrant workers packed up and traveled to New Church, Virginia. Among them were my mother and her new boyfriend, Claude. As it turned out, Claude was a very nice and charming man, but things got complicated when my dad found out that Claude and Ma would not only be in Virginia with us, but they we going to actually *live* in the same building with us. That was good news to us children, but it was unimaginable torture for my dad. That 'building' was actually a large single family house where rooms were rented out as accommodations for each migrant family.

I had never seen a house that gigantic in my entire life. It looked like a mansion. I thought to myself, "What a knock-out! We are going to live like kings and queens." The house was just across a railroad track. I loved trains and I had never lived near tracks before. The house had eighteen rooms, of which sixteen were bedrooms. It had one large kitchen which everyone shared, plus a bathroom and a half for the fifteen families that moved in. As luck would have it, Ma and Claude's room was right next to ours. This made my brothers and I feel like we had our mother back. Dad was not as pleased about the new living arrangements. It must have been unimaginably hard for him to have his wife living and sleeping with another man on the other side of the wall from where he stayed.

Our time in this house was magical for my brothers and me. Things were beginning to really look up for us again. We could visit my mother's room anytime we wanted. We spent many treasured and memorable times with her, building and working on our relationship. We began bonding again. I felt like God had answered my prayer. He had given me my mother back. She was now an integral part of my life. The other side of the coin was that we ended up spending less and less time with Daddy, who had remained a sure and constant support to us. I'm sure he felt abandoned by us, but kids just don't see things that way.

After a couple months of living next to each other, my mom and dad (along with her man friend Claude) began to talk. Things became less strained over time until their relationship seemed to grow into a friendship. Seeing things go so well, I thought, "God, you are so wonderful!" I was praying so hard that we could come together as a family again; however, this was a strange answer to my prayers. I never gave up the hope of my family reuniting again. Things could not get any better. We were really living now! My mom was in my life and I knew that nothing could take her away from us now. She was sober, she had a boyfriend, and she had her precious children.

Things were going so well...perhaps too well. These are often the times in life when the unexpected happens. Sometimes, tragedies arise out of the calm and threaten our very existence; even the steely hands of death will come to knock at our door. These are the times when we sometimes have the opportunity to cheat death and slam the door right in his face.

≈

One day that summer, Ma and I went to the little country store, which was directly across the railroad tracks a block or so from our house. The tracks were special to me. I loved to hear the train whistle blow and the rattling clackity-clacks as the wheels rolled over the gap in between the rails.

That day, my mother and I took a walk over to the store together to get some items that she needed. On our return in route to our house, there was a train sitting on the tracks just in front of us. It was not moving. After fifteen minutes had passed, the train still had not made any attempt to move. "This train could be here for hours!" Ma said. She was getting tired and very impatient. "This doesn't make sense, I'm going to go across." she said abruptly.

What she did next still boggles my mind to this day. Ma knelt down and began to crawl like a crab underneath the train. She ducked low, stretched each leg over the rail and scooted her body to follow. She edged and shuffled her little frame on her knees and on her "L" shaped arm to reach the other side. Suddenly, the train announced that it was going to move. The train began to vibrate and rattle, and along with the rumble, it blew its whistle loudly in one long hoot. The wheels started to turn slowly, one rotation and then another. The train was moving and my mother was underneath the belly of this iron freight!

I was still standing right where she had left me, and my instincts switched into alarm mode right away. "Ma! The train's moving!" I hollered as loudly as I could. Fear took over and I began yelling and screaming. I was in a panic. I could not see or hear Ma. The train now was roaring. It was so loud I could hardly hear myself screaming. I yelled "Ma the train is moving! Get from under the train!" Then I began to holler out, "Stop the train! Stop the train!" I bent down to see where she was. My eyes darted right and left like windshield wipers in heavy rain. *Where is she?* The train whistle huffed out another hoot and its wheels screeched as they turned slowly along the iron rail. Suddenly I spotted Ma. She was still under the train. "Hurry Ma, Hurry!" I could see her scurrying on her knees and scrambling towards the edge so she could get over the rail before the wheels would run over her body.

It is amazing how time will slow down during life's final moments, I think it means for us to take a mental photograph of the moment that life is about to be ended, because I saw the wheels of the train turning and rapidly coming upon my mother just as she swung her left leg over the rail. The wheel of the train was right upon Ma. For a devastating moment, I felt like I was the one underneath that train. I did not know if she had actually made it.

I had to wait for that train to pass, to find out whether Ma was alive. After an eternity of cars had passed, the train finally ended and I saw Ma standing on the other side of the rail. I dashed across to grab her waist all the while repeating, "Ma, you made it! You made it!" All I remember her saying was "Don't tell you father!" She may have just been thinking about hiding this crisis from Daddy but I was busy thanking Jesus for saving her life. The thought of losing Ma again, this time to death, was mental agony. Witnessing her dying in such a horrendous way would have taken my mind to a place of no return. I recognized God's hand in saving her life, even if she hadn't.

≈

Our new home came with many exploits but none nearly as adventurous as Ma escaping from under a moving train. Things were settling down comfortably, but the inevitable came. Dad announced that we had to move again. This time, we were going to Pennsylvania to pick potatoes. The migration of the buffalo had begun. The same Lumbee Indian families (along with the other families that were in Virginia) all came along. School was going to open soon so we enrolled the following week. After three months, the tribe all moved again... this time to Indiana.

Moving so often was devastating to me. I was torn away from friends just when I was beginning to bond with them. I was uprooted from teachers and classmates when I moved from school to school. It was like being on a merry-go-round; each ride was a new city or town. The inconsistencies made me long to get off the ride and plant my feet deeply on sturdy ground.

One afternoon, while in Indiana, my brothers and I eavesdropped on a conversation my father was having with one of the residents that lived in the house where we stayed. Dad was talking about moving again... but this time it was in the middle of the school year! I remember feeling like my heart was being torn in two. In the last 3 years, the school children of our migrant family clusters had not completed one school year in the same state and we were about to repeat that pattern again.

When dad actually sat the family down to talk, we discovered that the move was going to be back to Okeechobee. That talk dad had with us was very memorable because that was when he told us that we were finally going to settle down. Okeechobee would be the place where we would put down roots as a family. I cannot articulate the expression on dad's face. It was mixed with regret for having moved us so often and also with genuine hope of finally having some stability. As for my brothers and I, the thought of never moving again brought great elation and liberation to us. In Okeechobee, we knew quite a few people because we had been there long enough to get acquainted and make friends. I did enjoy the school and the teachers in Okeechobee and I would also be able to reunite with my classmates.

Little did I realize that in Okeechobee there was devastation like nothing I'd ever experienced before! It was waiting to crush and mangle my childhood; like that train that nearly steamrolled over Ma. Ma had missed that train; but the one that met me in Okeechobee ran over me, spun me around, and separated me into parts that only God Himself could ever put back together again.

Chapter 7

Asleep While the Wolf Prowls

~~~~~~

We finally got to Okeechobee, Florida. I remember pondering my father's words and his promise that we would never have to leave Okeechobee again. Such thoughts would cause the bells in my heart to ring for joy. I would automatically begin to sing with a smile plastered across my face every time I thought of returning home. Things moved slowly as we started settling down. In time, our family began to adjust to living in Florida again. I was delighted that we were back in Okeechobee just in time to celebrate my eleventh birthday. We moved into a small single family house where we didn't have to share the bathroom with fifteen other families. Having my family and everyone I loved around me made that birthday very exciting and very special indeed.

My father returned to work picking vegetables with Ma, Claude, and the other regulars. He also reverted back to being occupied with his own thoughts and spending little time engaged with us children. Meanwhile, my brothers and I would continue to spend as much time as possible with Ma and Claude. After about two months or so of being in Florida, Daddy seemed to check out from his duties as a father. The changes in him were so dramatic that I could hardly recognize the man I once knew to be a stable, reliable father, and one who was a leader of Christian values in our home.

My father took the elevator from non-drinker all the way to stone-cold alcoholic in the span of a couple months. For a man who was not accustomed to drinking alcohol, that was a feat indeed. He had the capacity of a thimble for alcohol. Just a couple of beers were enough to make him pass out cold. Once he was passed out, it was impossible to wake him up until the alcohol had worn off.

He reminded me so much of my mother when she used to drink. Alcohol had spun our lives out of control at one time and now it seemed that there would be detours that would carry my family down the path of destruction once again.

One Saturday afternoon, my father passed out on the couch, as per usual. Night soon fell and my brothers and I did what we customarily did, which was to wake him up so that he could get in his own bed and rest in a more comfortable position. I went to my bed as I usually did, but that night there was this hovering presence of evil. Before the night would end, it would turn out to be anything but usual.

≈

During the night, I was startled out of a deep sleep by the presence of someone breathing heavily in my face. The breathing was so rapid and deep that at first I thought that a wolf or some other animal was thirsty and panting for water. I was so petrified that my body actually could not move. I was literally paralyzed by fear. I could not even scream. This monster's breathing grew more labored and its moaning and groaning became louder. It began to slither all up and down my body. A pair of hands crept slowly across my chest, moving from my right breast to my left breast and then descending to my stomach. I tried once again to scream but before a sound could escape my lips, a hand which smelled of wood and cigarette smoke clamped over my mouth. I heard a voice lulling me low and harsh, "shushhhh!"

For a brief moment, I thought I recognized someone familiar, but before I could register a thought, monstrous hands moved down to my private parts and what felt like sharp knives pushed inside my little body. I withered and cried out under the hands which gripped my mouth, "Daddy!" I thought to myself, how could this be happening to me when my father was lying right in the next room?

My God how!? How God? "Oh God please help me, I'm dying!" I moaned out my prayer.

My little eleven year old body was in a state of shock due to the pain and agony of this assault. My mind couldn't understand that this was really happening to me. I had no control of this horrible situation. My dad was passed out from alcohol that had overpowered him. He was useless to help me as I was being overpowered by this monster just several feet from where he laid.

The wolf left just as suddenly as he came. I was left torn, bleeding, and trembling. Fear still gripped me and something else foreign mixed in; it was shame.

≈

When the light of day came, I could not recognize the wolf that came out last night to prey on the weak and helpless; slithering across the bedroom floor when all is silent and still; he strikes, raids and robs little girls of their souls by violating their bodies. This Dr. Jekyl had a real identity but he could not be identified in the light of day. Who or "what" was the predatory wolf that had attacked me last night?

Much to my horror, the wolf was in fact my brother Wade, now 17 and armed with a spirit of lust and sadism which he exhausted on my 11 year old body. What had happened that first night was only a prelude to what he would do to me for the next two years of my life. I was raped repeatedly, sodomized, and left lying in my own blood. When my shock wore off, I came to the realization that this was a purposeful assault that was planned and premeditated over an extensive period of time.

One night, I remember just being so splintered emotionally; the pain which wrenched my body and my heart was overwhelming. I braved repercussions of the threats from Wade and ran to the couch in the living room where my father was passed out. I began to shake him with all the strength that was left in me. I screamed and yelled. "Daddy! Daddy! Wake up! Please help me!" I kept shaking and pulling on him but he did not wake up. I reached for the string which turned on the overhead light, and in the glare of the light, I saw blood still running down my legs. It was all over my pink and floral nightgown that Daddy had bought just weeks before.

At that moment, I felt abandoned in the worse way by my father. My protector had let me down. I was trapped and imprisoned into a situation I had not asked for and I did not know where to turn for help. I was so frightened and terrified. I did not want to go back to bed because Wade would likely attack me again, if for no other reason, than to pay me back for trying to get help from dad. In my despair, I sat down on the couch beside my father until day break.

It was a relief to see the daylight. I was still mentally drained from trying to understand how my brother Wade became the monster that he was. I did not know him anymore. I lost my brother. When my father wakes up, I will have to tell him this boy that he raised is the wolf that attacks me during the nights while he sleeps.

Perhaps it was fear of what Wade would do to me in revenge or maybe fear that I would not be believed that kept me silent. Perhaps it was that I knew somewhere deep in my mind that dad would have surely killed Wade if he knew. Whatever it was, it won out over the desperation I had felt hours prior when I was trying to wake up dad. I said nothing.

By now, dad's drinking had become full blown and mom had returned to the bottle as well. Each time I saw Claude and her, they would be drunk. They would get so drunk that they would not even know their names, and they certainly didn't know mine. My brothers and I had seen men taking advantage of my drunken mother in various places and in various ways. Her "boyfriend" would be unaware of these vile acts even though men were in the bed next to him molesting Ma. It was us kids that had to shoo them off of her like one shooing vultures off of a dead carcass. This was becoming a way of life.

Alcohol had totally taken my dad. This meant that at night, Wade had no fear of dad waking up so his attacks became bolder. Each night, he would hold me down and do whatever he wanted to do with me. I would openly scream and try to get away but he would overpower me so much that I would practically pass out.

I begged dad to stop drinking but he couldn't seem to change his habit. Things were changing on the inside of me, however. I became filled with hate and I could not stand the sight of Wade. I didn't want to be in the same house with this maniac. I was too young to live on my own but I continuously asked God to deliver me.

The second year in Florida, when the school year began, I had an accident in gym class that (in a totally unimaginable way) became the stake that killed the werewolf who had been sucking my life away during my nights.

One day in Phys Ed, my classmates and I were playing a game on the playground called Crack the Whip. It's a game where kids would line up and link arms creating a chain representing the length of a whip. The head of the "whip" would pull along with the others to try and get someone disconnected. Those who fell away from the "whip" were out of the game. The last person standing was the winner. I was the head of the whip that day and I began to pull with all my might. I pulled so hard that I was the one to fall down, and the girl linked to me, Betty, fell on top of me. When I fell, my right leg went underneath me, and Betty, who was very heavy for a thirteen year old, fell right on top of that leg. I heard a cracking noise which was the sound of both the bones in my leg and my ankle breaking. Flares of pain shot through me as they rushed me to the hospital.

That day, I came home with a heavy plaster cast which went from the tip of my toes way up to the uppermost part of my thigh. As it turned out, that monstrosity of a cast became my best defense because it got in the way of Wade getting to me. After a couple inconveniences, he gave up on raping me in the nights because the cast was such an encumbrance. Wade moved out of our home shortly thereafter.

My life in Okeechobee was not what I had imagined. Though my family no longer moved from place to place anymore, my home-life was far from stable. My soul was so splintered. I was violated, marred, ashamed, fearful, and destroyed. I thought that I would never again be a normal person. My parents, who were once people who cared for me, were now absent from my life altogether. They had me left at the mercy of a ravenous wolf who had eaten away my childhood. Florida had become my worst nightmare and it wasn't until after a period of two years of hell that fate had looked kindly on me by breaking the bones in my leg. With Wade gone, I could finally breathe a little more comfortably and take in the briny air of Okeechobee's Lake which was a few miles from my house.

Chapter 8

The Day of the Smashed Windshield

My best friend was Kathy. I met her at Ma Brown's because her mother was a drinker like mine, and Kathy would have to go and get her mother out of the bar as well. Kathy and I had more in common than having drunks as mothers. Kathy's family also worked in the fields. It was there where we became fast friends. At times past, she would sleep over at my house which may not have been a good idea since Wade was still living there. More often than not, I would ask my dad for permission to sleep over at her house where it was safer.

Kathy and I were pretty much without parents so when my oldest sister Ruby (who was the first sibling to leave the nest), returned to Florida, both of us tried to worm our way into her home. Ruby was married at one time but now she was divorced and living with a guy named Jerry.

Ruby was ten years older than me, so Kathy and I thought that we could confide in her and that she would be a mother figure to us. We soon discovered that Ruby was not in a good place herself. Her boyfriend was one of those men who would get violent with her when he was drunk. He would hit Ruby and beat her up. One night, he turned his violence on me also. But, instead of hitting me with his fists, he used his brutish hands to cover my mouth so that I could not scream as he molested me. I felt like there was a sign on my head that said "Victim! Go ahead and do what you want to me". I wasn't going to let him get to me again. As a way of protecting myself, whenever I spent a night over at Ruby's house, I always took Kathy and we'd sleep together to watch out for Jerry.

≈

Ruby's life with Jerry was terrible. Even with me and Kathy there to encourage her, things got progressively worse. Jerry was a nasty kind of drunk. His temper would flare and he would beat on just about anyone or anything.

One day, Kathy and I were walking downtown. Okeechobee's downtown at that time was nothing more than a few stores with a park in the center to indicate some resemblance to an urban area. We walked by a store where Jerry was parked outside. He was drunk and cursing at somebody; we didn't know who. In his agitation, he swung around with his fist flying in the air and then brought it down on the windshield of someone's car. We were shocked. It was not just because he hit the windshield, but because the noise that his fist made on the windshield was thunderous! The glass crumbled into thousands of pieces and left a gaping hole where the windshield once was. Jerry had punched right through that glass and Kathy and I just looked at him with our jaws open. "What are you looking at?" Jerry barked at us. "Get in the car!" Like two spellbound idiots, Kathy and I got in.

Jerry drove us to his house. Once he demanded that we get out of his car, he drove off again to some local bar. Kathy and I were so relieved to get out of his car. The whole story of seeing Jerry smashing the windshield with his fist immediately scurried out of our mouths as we relayed it to Ruby. That story must have made an impression on Ruby because that evening she did something which I never thought that she would do. I know that after witnessing what Jerry did to that windshield, I got a different perspective on the beatings he'd given to her. It's a wonder that Jerry's fists had not scrambled Ruby's brains.

That evening, Jerry came home as drunk as a rat in a whiskey barrel. Jerry and Ruby had a big argument, which was not unusual.

Ruby threatened to leave. This was also not unusual since she was always threatening to leave. But when those words flew out of her mouth that evening, Jerry took his large switchblade knife and opened that six-inch blade. He calmly placed it by his left side as he reclined in the bed. He was very drunk but there was seriousness in that action that spoke volumes. Jerry eventually passed out on the bed. Afterwards, Ruby told me that she was *really* leaving. I never thought that she would have followed through with her threats. What Jerry did to the windshield must have made a serious impression on her, I thought.

We had to make sure that Jerry was truly asleep so for the next 45 minutes, Ruby, Kathy and I made sounds by doing odd things like coughing loudly, stomping our feet on the floor, and feigning calling each other's name out loud. We even bent right over his head, calling "Jerry, wake up!"

Thankfully, Jerry was passed out as cold as the blade of that knife by his side, because he certainly would have killed my sister if he woke up to see what we were doing. Ruby already had some clothes and other things packed and hidden away in garbage bags. We loaded them up and darted off in her old Nova convertible. "Go! Go! Go!" was something specific I remembered both of us saying because we were taking our lives in our hands and this was our only window of escape. We had to get out before it closed or else my sister would be leaving in a body bag instead of that Nova.

I'm sure that I was breathing while we were in the house pulling out garbage bag after garbage bag of her things but I was not aware that I was. We were prowling like burglars, taking each bag past the bedroom where Jerry was laying down. It seemed that we were holding our breaths the entire time, even when we finally drove off. My sister's head was facing forward at the driver's wheel but all Kathy and I could do was continuously look back to see whether Jerry had woken up at the last second and was following us.

We stopped at a gas station to put our frazzled minds back in place and to gather our wits about us. Then, we made a beeline straight to North Carolina where one of my mom's sisters, Aunt Shorty, lived. I wasn't quite sixteen years old at that time, but having that experience of running away from Jerry and escaping a possible fatality, seemed to age me a little more.

As it turned out, North Carolina was only a pit-stop, a place which served as a safe haven away from Jerry. While in North Carolina, Ruby reconnected with her ex-husband, and after a few months of courtship via the telephone, he persuaded her to move to Maryland. Like two peas in a pod, Kathy and I followed right along with her.

Chapter 9

Maryland: Home of the Firsts

I didn't particularly care for Maryland because I wasn't there by choice, but I was grateful to leave my past of abuse and drama behind in Florida. I did not want any of the demons of my past to follow me to Maryland so I became very withdrawn. Kathy was the only one who I truly related with since Ruby was very much into her new role as wife to her ex - now current husband. I was now sixteeen and legally qualified to work, so I got a job working at a department store called Woolworth's. Woolworth's was my first real job, and at sixteen, other 'firsts" were waiting for me.

Around that time, Ruby heard that a lot of Lumbee Indians had migrated to Baltimore from North Carolina. We lived in Oxon Hill; a racially-mixed community south of Washington, D.C. The area was dotted with apartment buildings. Many apartment complexes were being built at that time and we were fortunate to rent a modern apartment in a complex that had a swimming pool. Oxon Hill is about an hour's drive from Baltimore and we began to make regular visits to Baltimore on the weekends. Over a period of time, Ruby reunited with former friends from our region of Lumberton, North Carolina.

Before long, Ruby became a Baltimore regular. She began hanging out with her new friends, who were partying folks, and she also became a regular at a local juke joint called the Volcano. Ruby's husband, who was a hard-working provider, didn't mind her going to have some fun in Baltimore because he was usually too exhausted to come along.

Kathy and I would follow Ruby to Baltimore, but because we were under age, we were not allowed to enter the bar. Kathy and I would mainly hang around outside of the bar entertaining ourselves with whatever time-wasting ideas we could think of. Mainly, we'd listen to music in the car or just talk with whoever would leave the bar to get some fresh air outside. Not everybody came out for fresh air. Some came out to smoke. One such person was a young, handsome, Lumbee Indian guy who would spend time talking with us. His name was Romeo and his twenty-one years had turned him into a young man whose piercing green eyes, good looks, and charm, did his name justice.

My friendship with Romeo was initially limited to the weekends when we would visit the Volcano, but after about two months, Romeo began coming down to Oxon Hill to see me. Romeo's visits on the weekends made me feel important…important enough that a man would come to see me. Romeo made me feel like a whole new person. My hair, my shape, my eyes, my mouth, my nose - my entire body, suddenly turned into a thing of wonder and beauty, because Romeo continuously told me how pretty I was. I was mesmerized by his attention and it didn't take long before I fell in love for the first time.

Romeo was very attentive. We would walk together holding hands; I'd let him put his arm around my shoulder and I'd feel so safe and so loved. One evening, while in Baltimore outside the Volcano bar, amidst the ambiance of the grey sidewalk, street lights, and the loud noises of rowdy drinkers who came out for a smoke, Romeo turned my face towards him and kissed me like I had never been kissed before. I really was never kissed before. That first kiss that I experienced with Romeo, transported me from outside the Volcano to a place where I thought had to be Heaven.

Having kissing sessions with Romeo began to make our relationship look more and more like a baseball game. He would try to hit a homerun while I would try to get him to strike out. He asked me to have sex with him in as many creative ways as he could imagine.

He'd say that I did not love him as much as he loved me: because if I loved him, I would share my body with him. After a while, asking turned to begging, and when I still would not give in to him, his begging turned to threats. Dodging his wiles was becoming harder and harder. He threatened to leave me by saying that he would take back his high school ring. He said that ring was his promise that he would marry me and that having sex with him was okay since we would be together for the rest of our lives. I truly believed that Romeo and I would be together for the rest of our lives.

It was in my sister's house that I had my first sexual experience with Romeo. It was like taking a fast train ride through all the ghost towns of molestations and victimizations that I had once known. I felt so ashamed on so many levels and I vowed that I would never voluntarily put myself through that experience again. Four weeks later, I missed my period.

In addition to finding myself unmarried and pregnant at seventeen years old, my whole past came back to haunt me. I felt like I violated my own self by voluntarily laying down with someone who was not my husband, and of all places, in my sister's house! I thought of the times when my brother had raped me and covered me with shame, but this time I had brought the shame upon myself. I thought of my mother whom I'd seen violated by men because she let alcohol bring her to a place of abasement. She and my father had both scandalized our family and the Lumbee community and now I had joined the ranks of the debauched Hunts. I felt unclean and I hated myself. I wanted to leave my place of shame, so without giving Ruby any reasons why, I left Maryland and moved back to Aunt Shorty's house - our place of refuge in North Carolina.

I took shame with me and fear came along as well. A curse that was lurking in the shadows of my ancestry had taken a hold of me and it had me bound secure with chains of hopelessness. This generational predator which had grabbed my heels in my younger years now seized me in my young adult life. I had seen this curse take over the life of my parents, my sister, and my brother, and now my life would be no better than the rest.

Chapter 10

Married Life: The War of the Hunts

Romero followed me to North Carolina after a few weeks. As it turned out, Romeo was no stranger to the little town where Aunt Shorty lived because his parents also lived there. It's a small world. We got married a couple weeks later. That was one step I could take to help save my reputation. We moved into his mother's house.

Three days after my marriage, the pattern for the rest of my married life started. Romeo would leave on a Friday afternoon and wouldn't come home until Monday night. That was the first time I heard what became his mantra: "I got tied up with the boys". My response should have been "Did *she* have a full deck?", but I was too tired from struggling to dodge the bullets from his mother's constant accusations of me sleeping with her sixty year old husband. That woman was a vacuum who sucked up all the negative things which life had to offer. Filled with hate and meanness, she'd chase her little husband all over the house cussing him in ways that would make any sailor blush.

After a few months, Romeo got a job working a couple hours' drive away from home. That job became an excuse for him to be gone all week. He'd come home on Friday evenings, take a shower, and leave to be with his "boys". I was left behind with the mother-in-law from Hades. In order to find a way out of her house, I got a job at a chicken farm cleaning chickens to get extra money. That chicken money helped. One month before having my baby, I was able to move into a broken-down trailer whose next stop would have been the city dump...if I had not rescued it.

That trailer was an escape from my demon-in-law, but now I was alone most of the time because Romeo was still a rolling stone. I was left alone with my new born baby, asking myself, *why was this man not respecting me*? I wasn't respected in his mother's house. I'm not even respected in my own house! He didn't respect me as a person, as his wife, or as the mother of his child. I had reached my boiling point.

I threatened to leave and go back to Baltimore with my baby and to never let Romeo know where we were. I was very serious but Romeo begged me not to leave. He promised me that both of us could start anew in Baltimore. He went ahead of us to Baltimore and got a job hanging drywall. After working for about six weeks, he found a two room apartment and sent for us. My eight month stay in that trailer had ended.

The two-room apartment was already occupied with tenants who did not pay rent. They were roaches. This place was where the roaches returned when they left from vacation at the Roach-Motel.® When I turned on the lights, I would actually hear these armies of roaches scatter into the shadows. They had no boundaries. They'd crawl on me and they'd crawl on the baby in the bassinet. My nights were spent on guard duty watching my baby to make sure that roaches didn't crawl on her. I had to constantly wash all her things because those unwelcomed tenants would pollute everything. That apartment made me long to return to the glamor of the trailer-house in North Carolina.

Having a house full of roaches wasn't all bad because they became my familiar companions since Romeo was rarely in the house with us. He was still just using the home as a pit-stop. Romeo became increasingly disrespectful. If he treated a dog the way he treated me, he would have been arrested for animal cruelty. There was nothing I said or did that pleased him. Put-downs, insults, and cussing were his regular form of communicating with me. I could hardly turn around without him pushing me. That was his way of provoking an argument. I felt so demeaned and debased, and Romeo's mistreatment only intensified my despair. He wanted me to have nothing and he wanted me to be a nobody.

My life as a young adult was so tragic that it had wiped out the horrible memories of the molestations of my childhood and the memories of what alcohol had done to my family. I needed to get a new life. I wanted friends, I wanted fun, and I wanted some degree of happiness. My desire was soon satisfied and it was closer than I thought.

≈

I met one of Romeo's cousins who lived up the street from me. She seemed to enjoy life and I was glad to have her as a new friend. One evening, she invited me out to my first concert. We went to see the Chavis Brothers who were playing in a club about seven miles from my house. I knew Romeo didn't want me out enjoying myself without his permission so I was very nervous. I was also very timid; I felt that others could see my shame. I willed myself to walk without wobbling as my knees were actually knocking together. Also, I had never taken a drink before, not even when I would hang out outside of the Volcano with Kathy and Romeo.

That night, I discovered that one drink can change a person. My first drink was a Singapore Sling and that alone was enough to make me forget Romeo and the other cockroaches at home. Before the night was over, I was on the dance floor celebrating the freedom I felt while listening to the Elvis-beat of the Chavis Brothers rock-n-roll band, and sipping my Singapore Sling.

I was not about to give up this ticket to freedom that I experienced that night; never mind that it came with a costly price tag. The change was gradual, but like cold water on top of a hot flame, the temperature will eventual rise to a boiling point. Within a period of months, I had turned into a regular member of the partying bar scene in Baltimore. Things between Romeo and I had also risen to a boiling point. He hated 'his' woman to be out from under his control, even if it was alcohol and partying that was now taking control of me. Coming home with alcohol on my breath would anger him to the point that, one night as I lay in bed, he hocked and spat every bit of phlegm which his lungs could bring up...right in my face!

Chapter 11

Spiraling Downward

~~~~~

That action triggered every dormant feeling of anger, resentment, and hate for the life of hell which I've been through with Romeo. I was so angry that I took all my rage out in the kitchen. I flung plates and pans against the wall and shattered the window with the cast-iron skillet. Romeo was so mad that I ruined *his* house that he went and got his 38 caliber handgun from underneath the mattress. It wasn't until he had placed the cold barrel squarely on my right temple that I bounced back into sobriety. I snapped into flight mode and dashed out that front door, and I shot down the street like I was a bullet ricocheting from that gun. To this day, I could not tell you whether I ran outside in my flimsy nightgown or in my skimpy underwear.

That fateful night was the beginning of a new era in my marriage. That episode opened the door to more volatile chapters. I was under a type of house-arrest indicted by Romeo while he continued his life of leaving me and our little girl behind. He enforced his verdict with violent threats and physical attacks by pushing me around and threatening to kill me.

About the time of our daughter's third birthday, my sister Sylvia came from North Carolina to live in Baltimore. She was having difficulty adjusting to the change of the city. For a reprieve, she would drive down to North Carolina every three weeks or so. Romeo allowed me and our daughter to go with her. I felt like a cadet getting leave from boot camp. I'd drop off my daughter at my aunt's house and head to one of the juke-joints which catered to a lot of Lumbee Indian customers. I wanted to celebrate my freedom. Even though, like my father, I had a low tolerance for alcohol, I would drink until I lost all my inhibitions and then emerge as the flame which would light up the bar and bring the party to life.

One day, after returning back to Baltimore, I walked in my house to find Romeo sitting knee-locked with some lady at the kitchen table. They were holding hands. It seemed that we both were living secret lives.

Also, about that time, my brother Wade (whom I had hoped never to hear from again) called me to give me the type of news which should have stopped me from my relationship with alcohol. My mom, who had remained under the blanket of drunken stupor, was hit by a car while she staggered across the road on her way home from a bar. The car had thrown her body 20 feet in the air. Did I expect a different end to the life of one who was a whore to the bottle?

I should have been more broken-up and sobered by this news, but the bottle which had been the inspiration behind my mother's death, was holding me too tightly by now. During that entire weekend of my mom's memorial, I partied like I was immortal because her death allowed me to be on furlough from Baltimore.

The problems in my life were now getting so out of control that the alcohol couldn't even mask my pain and make me forget my troubles at home any longer. Romeo's cover behind which he had hidden his customary "time with the boys" had been completely blown off that night when I saw him at the kitchen table holding hands with this other woman. One night, I decided to go out to party when I was under "house-arrest". While driving to the bar, I saw him in his truck kissing this woman at a stoplight. Rage took over and I purposed that he would die that night. When he came home, I had a butcher-knife in my hand, which I was determined to plunge downward and lodge in his body. He happened to call before returning home that night and when I told him what I had seen, he told me that the person I saw was another guy who had borrowed his truck. His excuse didn't deter my intentions.

Romeo's survival instinct must have picked up that I was serious because it took him three days of begging and promising a new beginning for us before he came back in our home. As it turned out, his purpose for weaseling his way back into the house was to get back at me. He cleaned out all our furniture while I was out of the house so that my daughter and I didn't even have a mattress to sleep on.

I thought that I was capable of killing Romeo before but that butcher knife had to go in retirement because I needed a fresh and a fast way to finally rid myself of this person who continued to hurt me so badly. An inquiry from a neighborhood kid and seventy-five dollars brought a gun into my hands within 12 hours. Romeo had taken me to a place where I believed that life in prison was better than the life I had living with him.

≈

For two days, I sat on the other side of the front door with that gun in my hand, mentally willing Romeo to come home so that the three steps it took for him to get fully in the house would be his last.

The second night, I went to bed with anger, not just from what he had done to me in the past, but because he didn't come home and I didn't even get the satisfaction of shooting him. That night, I dreamt that Romeo had walked in the front door and I was sitting in the chair with my legs crossed. I looked up at him, aimed the gun at the middle of his chest and shot him without saying a word. He fell over backwards and blood was all over the front of his shirt. I got up and looked at him. Instantly, fear of what I had done took over. I started to scream. Somehow, I knew the paramedics were on their way and the police were right behind them. I was going to prison for sure. I woke up.

That dream shocked me into reality. The thought of actually killing someone and going to prison was more than I could deal with. The next day, I gave the gun back to my "contact" and told him to get rid of it.

Romeo did come home that week. He once again did the begging routine and I once again gave in. The cycle of Romeo's adulterous escapades, violence and reconciliation continued. This pattern of behavior was such a stronghold, that even the fact that I caught him in bed with my neighbor (whom I beat so badly with an iron) didn't stop the trend.

Chapter 12

Can't Fake the Real Thing

One day, Romeo came back to my front door after a two-week absence with the same routine of begging, "Baby, please let me in. I love you. We can do this thing. I know you need me...." and the like. But *this* time, he surprised #me with a new story. "Baby, I got saved! I gave my life to the Lord! I love you more now than I ever did 'cause I got Jesus!"

Romeo kept coming back and I was desperate for anything that would help. My spirit was so depleted and I was so mentally drained that I chose instead to hope in this new thing that he said he had. As a result, I let him back in our house. Within two weeks, I discovered that this "Jesus experience" he claimed he had, was just a temporary covering. Romeo told me that he wanted to move out and "find himself". As it turned out, the "self" he left to find was another woman whom he moved in with.

I remember other people who had claimed to know Jesus and who had disappointed me. I remember my once strong, faith-filled mother, my once church-going leader of a father; and now my husband who said he had some spiritual experience, but whose faith lasted about as long as it took for paint to dry.

On the other hand, I could not deny that there were also other people I knew who seemed to have a genuine life of peace and joy and who remained constant in their faith in Jesus. I remembered my

Aunt Arretta who had taken my siblings and me in her home while dad and mom had gone to Okeechobee.

On the evening of my thirty-ninth Birthday, I went to a bar in Mt. Pleasant, Maryland with about fifteen of my friends. The evening started out with fun and lots of laughter. I was always the life of the party when I drank. "Loretta's in the house!" they would all say. I was on my second beer when out of nowhere my laughter turned into crying. I cried so long and so hard that it passed the point of embarrassment. I couldn't control it no matter how hard I tried. I just had to give in to it. As strange as that was, it was my friends' response to my crying that was even more bizarre. They started laughing at me. The more I cried, the more they laughed. The harder I cried, the louder they laughed. I had no particular reason to be crying but I knew that the desperation and the pain within my soul had crossed over into my consciousness and had broken past all my barriers of sociability and decorum. I couldn't get a grip on my emotions, and intellectually, I couldn't understand why my friends would see my plight as funny. I had no control over what was happening to me, and I had no handle on my life. Apparently, I had control over myself either. I could not turn off the value to my tears and I continued weeping even as I lay in my bed that night.

≈

The next morning, I was sitting in a church in downtown Baltimore, where I knew some Lumbee Indians were attending. The songs and the sermon I heard just caused more leaks in my soul and I cried even harder.

I kept going to church however, because I knew somehow that I was in the right place. I was so relieved to be around people who were not in a smoke-filled bar and in a place where alcohol, sex, and vomit were a part of the scene. In fact, the "crying in my beer" night was the last time I ever went into a bar.

One Tuesday evening I heard a message called "Missing Jesus". I remember this message so clearly and I will *never* forget the date. It was May 25th 1993. I was sitting four rows from the back having worked my way up from the last row over a period of weeks. The weather outside was light and breezy, but the atmosphere inside the church was charged that night. The preacher was telling the story about Jesus walking on the water. "When Jesus was walking towards the disciples and He told Peter to come, Peter didn't have to do anything but go!" He was an energetic man and he was charged as he spoke. "Peter didn't have to bring anything with him. Peter didn't have to clean up first. Peter didn't say, 'Lord, I can't come to you because I'm not perfect'. Peter just got out of the boat and came to Jesus." He continued his message. "Things didn't look pretty for Peter. There was water all around him. The wind was blowing and the waves were rolling, but Peter got out of his boat and came to Jesus." He slapped the podium and he raised his voice a couple of notches. "Jesus is calling you!" He said that with such conviction. "Your life doesn't have to be perfect for you to come to Jesus. You don't have to clean up first. Your life may be like the sea that was all around Peter. Your life may be rough. Storms might have swept over you. Some of you have been throw major hurricanes at sea. But, don't look to fix up. Don't look to clean up. Don't look to getting it all together first. None of that can happen without Jesus!" He was preaching more forcefully now and when he said "Jesus", it was as if he brought a hammer right down into my soul. He moved from behind the podium and started scanning the audience. His eyes landed squarely on me. I didn't know how he found me so far in the back, but I *felt* that he was talking directly to me. "Matthew 6:33 says, 'Seek first the Kingdom of God and all these things shall be added to you.' Many times we say, 'Jesus, I'll come to you after I clean up my act'. 'Jesus, I'll come to you after I start living right'. But the Bible says that these things can't happen until we seek Jesus *first*. The thing that we need to do *first* is come to Jesus. *Jesus* is the first step in getting our lives right. *Jesus* is what's missing!"

    I was not aware of anyone else that was in the church. I listened intently as he spoke just to me. His voice raised a couple octaves as he spoke, "Romans 10:9 and 10 say, 'That if you confess with your mouth, "Jesus is Lord," and believe in your heart that God raised Him from the dead, you will be saved. For it is with your heart that you believe and are justified, and it is with your mouth that you confess and are saved'."

A light switch flipped on in my brain. It didn't occur to me to come to Jesus *first*. I had so many issues in my life and because I grew up in Church, I didn't want to come with all my mess. I was shattered in pieces because of Wade had assaulted my body and fragmented my soul. I had no sound identity because Romeo had berated me and chipped away the good things I ever felt about myself. I was empty and hollow inside and all the alcohol and partying didn't fill my void. I was lonely and my friends didn't understand how needy and desperate I was; they had all laughed at me. How was I going to fix my life?! Church could fix me. Church was my new hangout and the people at church were my new friends; but on the inside, I was the same desperate young woman. It became abundantly crystal to me that what I was missing in my life was Jesus!

"Come to Jesus Loretta" I could hear that voice whispering in my heart. "Come to Jesus." The words speak over and over again. "He's your first step. He's what's missing" Like Peter, I was tempted to look at the crashing waves of life's problems which surrounded me, but I decided that I would keep my eyes on Jesus and step off my boat. The preacher said, "Does anyone here want to come to Jesus today?" He didn't have to ask twice. My heart was racing to Jesus, even though I calmly got up and walked down that aisle, to the altar up front.

"Jesus...Jesus...Jesus" was all I managed to say. I gave Him everything I knew myself to be. I vomited every disgusting feeling that was in my soul. I felt so sorry for all my sin and for all my mess. "Jesus...Jesus....Jesus", I was begging Him to take me. I wanted nothing left of me. I wanted all of HIM.

I felt a huge burden lifted off of me. I felt like I had been carrying a sack of bricks on my back and Jesus took it away. I felt so light. I could almost see a giant brick wall which was separating me and God crumbling to pieces before my eyes. I felt like I was dipped in water that had miraculously cleansed my insides.

I understand what Adam must have felt like when God blew His very own breath into the clay that he was before, and gave him life. I felt like God bent down over the lifeless, hardened, clay which was my soul - and breathed into me. I rose up and left that altar a brand new person.

Chapter 13

Tie the Knot and Break the Chain

Around the same time that I found God, Romeo found a new way to get close to me again. Like a bad rash, he was persistent in his pursuit of getting back into my life. Romeo was like a cross-country truck driver. He had to be constantly on the move, but he needed a steady pit-stop to change and refresh himself for his journey. Romeo was accustomed to my house being his pit-stop and he didn't want to give up his favorite location. Since he'd left, I had gotten myself a new apartment, and I had made up my mind that he had to get another hangout; because my rest-stop was closed.

I soon learned that the Church had expectations of married couples: mainly that they remain married and living together, regardless of extenuating circumstances like repeated adultery and abuse. In fact, I was barely off my knees with my new found experience of faith, when someone said to me, "Now you can get back together with your husband!"

Romeo was now among the church members claiming to be a Christian. Now that I became a Christian myself, he pursued me in earnest. He told me how much he had changed and I assumed that what I experienced on that miraculous Tuesday evening was also what he had experienced. In addition to Romeo, people at church also kept telling me that God forgave me — so I need to forgive him, implying that taking him back would be the only evidence of me forgiving Romeo. The weight of church doctrine (however misapplied or misinterpreted) solidified my decision and within the space of a week of my new found experience, Romeo moved into my apartment with me. As it turned out, that decision sent me to a place in my marriage where I could only describe as a hefty slice of heaven.

≈

I knew that a miracle had happened. I had more joy in my life than I had ever experienced before. Everything was washed away and wiped clean! Every bad memory erased and every wound healed. It felt good to finally let go of past baggage and not live with the burden of hurts, unforgiveness, and fear. Being in such a place of freedom, I allowed myself to trust Romeo to the fullest, and I experienced life as his wife in a way which I never experienced before.

We would walk together holding hands and we sat side by side in church. That was the best time that we ever had in all the thirteen years which we had been married. Romeo was a new man. He came home every day after work. He would call me two or three times a day. When he came home, we would go on dinner dates. Even when I cooked at home, it was like we were on a date. Sometimes, he would fire up the grill and cook steaks for me. He would also light candles and we would bask in each other's company by the glow of candlelight. He would rub my feet! I was on the honeymoon that I never had. One time, he even picked me up and carried me to bed.

We would study the Bible together, and we would pray together during the week when Romeo came home after work. I felt like I had finally gotten ahold of the brass-ring of life, and though our beginning was rough, we would walk the latter miles of our relationship in unity and love. I thought, *"Change my name to Juliet, my Romeo has finally found me!"*

I praised God for this new life, I praised God for changing my Romeo, and I thanked Him for showing me the love of a man, which was something I never experienced before in my life. Who else could make such a change happen? I would just sit on the sofa, amazed that Romeo was sitting right by my side, night after night, rubbing my feet and reading me Bible stories. This was better than any fairy tale. I had my true love, and he was my own husband whom God had changed from an Ogre into Prince Charming.

One day, my Romeo came home and said that he had to talk to me. I was pleased to sit and talk with my man, who had called me that day just to say, "I love you and I love loving you." We sat together at the kitchen table and he looked down on the empty plate in front of him. He looked so pained that my heart went out to him. "What's wrong?" I asked. I was gravely concerned after seeing the forlorn expression on his downcast face.

≈

He hardly looked up at me as he started to speak, "I don't know *who* I am anymore. I'm so confused. I really don't understand what is happening to me". He continued, "This hurts me so much more than it hurts you." I could see an expression of pain along his furrowed brows and my heart went out to him, even though I didn't understand what he meant when he said he didn't know who he was anymore. Was he emotionally lost, or was he experiencing some identity crisis? Poor Romeo, how can I help him find himself?

I remained quiet as Romeo continued. "I love you so much. Baby, you know I love you, but I can't take it anymore. I am leaving. I'm moving out!"

If an alien had landed in my kitchen and beamed me up in his spaceship to give me a brain transplant, I couldn't have been more shocked! That might well have happened, because I just could not make sense of what Romeo just shared with me. My mind could not function properly. Scrambled thoughts kept darting across my mind. Conflicts and dilemmas intermingled and nothing was computing or making sense. The computer of my mind had crashed. Did he just say that he's leaving!? Someone doesn't leave in the middle of a fairy tale - especially not in the "happily ever after part"! My world full of "dreams finally come true" crashed and shattered into a million pieces.

That very same evening, Romeo left. I begged him not to go, not to pack his things. I pleaded with him to stay with me and to continue to experience the joy which we had known in the past few months of our marriage. I implored him to look to Jesus and to pray. I dropped to my knees and I prayed like I had never prayed before but Romeo was as unmoved as the hardened heart of a dead corpse. He walked out of the room and as he headed for the front door, my parting words were, "One day, it won't hurt anymore!"

≈

I thought that the people at church would understand what had happened to me but the only thing that mattered to them was that I was a married woman separated from my husband. They told me that I needed to go back to my husband-never mind that he was the one who left me…again. They didn't treat me the same way as they did when Romeo and I were the picture-perfect couple. In fact, I was now seen as a rebellious and disobedient wife; and though I desperately needed comfort, I felt more burdened and loaded down.

About three weeks after Romeo left me, comfort came. It came from a stranger who was passing through our church. He was a visiting pastor who was there for a week. I made an appointment and had my first formal counseling experience. This pastor actually opened up the Bible and showed me places like Matthew 19:9 that explain how Romeo's continuous adultery and immorality was a deal breaker in our marriage covenant.

He told me that God is a righteous and holy God. He said that God was not a religious God who is not fooled or impressed by religious appearing people. He also showed me Matthew 7: 16-19 in the Bible that tells me how I can judge whether a person is a real Christian or a fake Christian. The Bible says that we can make a judgment by looking at the fruit they produce or the lifestyle they live. This is kind of like biting down on a piece of jewelry to see if it's pure gold or some other metal covered with shiny yellow paint. I already knew all the rottenness that was the real Romeo even though the people at church were impressed with his nice-guy exterior.

The pastor also showed me I Corinthians 5:17 that states that if an unbelieving husband leaves, his wife is permitted to just let him leave. I am under no obligation to take him back in my house. God prefers that I live in peace. I began wondering why I would never just let Romeo leave. Leaving me was one of the things which Romeo did best throughout the thirteen years of our marriage. I got to thinking that maybe I should give God's Word a try.

Finally the pastor gave me a piece of personal advice. He said that Romeo would come back and ask to live in my house, just like he had done in the past. But when he does, I am to put my foot down, take a stand, and not let him back in my house. He was living with another woman and if he wanted to come to my house for any reason, he should call and make an appointment first. The pastor also said that Romeo would do one of two things: either he'd repent and change or he'd leave and never return. I just needed to take my stand for righteousness. When I left that counseling session, I felt like chains dropped off of my body and I could actually float home. Who knew that the answer to all my "Romeo" questions were in the Bible all along!

≈

Just like clockwork, the next day at 6:00am, Romeo showed up at my house! I peeped out from behind my bedroom curtain and saw him standing on the steps by the front door. My heart began to pound with excitement, and my hope of a future of what we used to have, returned with full force. He knocked at my door. I kept rehearsing all that the pastor had told me. I had to keep my desire to let him in at bay. He kept knocking and knocking but I would not answer the door. Next, the phone began to ring. It kept ringing and ringing and ringing. My hands were itching to pick it up and my ears were longing to hear that things were finally going to be okay between us. But, I held on to what that pastor had told me.

After about 15 minutes, Romeo had moved to the back door. He began banging and banging. I kept thinking that perhaps this time would be the time when he has really changed. I wondered whether he had realized how good things were and how things could be again. I thought, "Maybe, he came to his senses" but I kept remembering what the pastor said.

Soon, Romeo began to holler and beg me to open the door. "Baby, let me in! I know you're in there! Open the door!" He was banging so hard that I thought he would break the glass of the door. I was beginning to be embarrassed and fearful that the neighbors would call the police because of the racket he was making, so I ran upstairs, hoisted the bedroom window and stuck my head out. I hollered down, "Hey you, stop banging on *my* door or I'm gonna call the police! You don't live here anymore. This is *not* your house. You don't pay bills here. Get outta here!" I felt good when I heard such words coming out of my mouth. For the first time, I wasn't the one being rejected.

"This is my house!" he hollered back. "Not anymore" I yelled in reply. I sounded brave on the outside, but on the inside, I knew that I was addicted to Romeo like I used to be addicted to those cancerous cigarettes; one puff, and I'd be sucked back in all over again, and that would be the end of my freedom.

Then, Romeo began to take the romance route. "I love you", he kept declaring. "I know you got somebody in that house but he don't love you like I do." I replied, "I'm glad he don't." I was becoming smarter and more empowered by the second.

Romeo had to up the ante with another move. He groaned aloud and fell over on the grass clutching his chest. "My chest, I think I'm having a heart attack!" He acted just like Redd Foxx from "Sanford and Son". I hollered down like a true Florence Nightingale, "You want me to call 911!?" When he saw that his ploy didn't work, he decided to play the religious card. "We can make it work baby. We both got God in our lives!" God plus a heart attack was his double whammy maneuver and it almost snagged me.

My heart was bursting out of my chest by that time, and my mind was going back and forth, wanting to take him back. However, somewhere deep down inside a tiny voice of truth was making me aware of its presence. It reminded me that this was an enemy trying to trick me. For the first time in my marriage, I listened. "Look! Get out of *my* yard 'cause if you don't, I'm going to call the police!" and with that, I shut the window with all the conviction that I could muster.

≈

I never looked back.

≈

That was the last image I have of Romeo because from that day to the present, I never saw him again. His schemes involved the church members and he even went to the pastor of the church and asked him to talk to me about *my* mistake of not letting him back in my life. He wooed and charmed the ladies at my church with his good husband routine and they would bombard me with scriptures encouraging me to go back to him like a good Christian wife. It was as if Romeo had invited the whole church in my backyard and they were all banging on my door. I finally had to make the decision that Romeo was not the only one I had to shut the window on. I went to another church where Romeo and the people he influenced were no longer a part of my life.

Chapter 14

Healing and Wholeness

I moved to another apartment and I didn't tell anybody where I lived. My experience with God was so real to me. I resolved to let God take control of my life rather than letting other people and circumstances determine how I lived. In doing so, I discovered many things, most of which were things within my own self. It is amazing how my past impacted most of the choices that I made. The tapestry of my life had so many dark threads woven into it. When I looked on the backside of it, I would see a bunch of threads, dark and knotted up into an ugly mess. But God gave me new eyes and taught me how to look at the tapestry front side up. Front side up, I can see that those dark threads which look so ugly on the back-side are vital parts in the grand scheme of things. Those dark threads make the lighter and more colorful parts of my tapestry shine and stand out. I began to appreciate the beautiful picture which is my life, woven together to create a portrait of God's purpose for me.

I began to see tragedies from my past and trials which I have encountered in an entirely new way. One such trial which would have overcome me, but for God's grace, was the discovery that I had breast cancer just a few months after I closed the door on Romeo. My journey started out with a feeling of discomfort in my left breast. My doctor rightfully thought it was only fatty tissue but a biopsy revealed that a cancer nodule was hiding behind it. When I got the news, I had one of those experiences where some people say that they have right before they die. My whole life flashed before my eyes. That is so cliché, but truly, every memory from my past came back to my mind in rapid succession. Flash! Flash! Flash! Memories fired across my mind like scenes in a movie.

I was at work when the doctor called to deliver the news and I had to hold it together but when I got home, I slid on my knees to the side of my bed like I was sliding into home-plate; I was desperate to get in touch with God. I told God that He is now in control of my life and whatever happens to me, it's on *Him*. I told Him that this is going to be between Him and me. And since I had shut myself off from most people from my past anyway, that promise wasn't hard to keep.

I never told anyone about the chemotherapy I was doing. I bought a wig that looked exactly like my own hair. Like a premonition, every strand of my beautiful thick hair fell out in the shower the very day that I brought the wig home. Apart from the medical people involved in my treatment, no one else knew.

During that time of going through cancer treatments, I experienced a season that can only be described as major and radical psychotherapy. God was my psychotherapist and the Bible was the manual He used to guide me through the process of change. I was a broken chard of a soul, and while I was doing what I needed to do physically to rid myself of this invasion of cancer in my body, God was doing spiritual chemo to bring wholeness to my damaged soul.

Every two weeks for a period of three hours, I would go to the hospital to get very potent and aggressive chemo; but every evening after work, I went to my "counseling appointment". I would grab my Bible and spend time in serious therapy with God for about five hours. Apparently, the ravages and plundering that had eroded my soul through the rapes, rejections, abandonment, alcohol, and wounds were more damaging to my soul than any cancer could be to my body.

One of things I asked God for when I found out that I was going to do chemo and radiation is that I did not want to get sick. I'm glad He answered my prayer. I'd like to think that it was because I had so much sickness on the inside of me that dealing with that was enough.

God was opening my eyes to many things. He showed me that He was cutting dead parts off of me, like a gardener who prunes off dead limbs from a tree so that it can grow new and fuller branches. Sometimes, I could practically feel the pain from God's cutting. Most of the time however, I would feel overwhelmed with the revelation of how much God loved me. I would cry aloud sometimes because I could not understand how He could love me to the extent that He did. I could feel liquid love pouring into a cavity within me that seemed desperately empty and ravenous. The more He gave me, the more I wanted. Sometimes, I was so overwhelmed with God's love that I would just bawl. My friend from work would call me to go out (other than the fact that I didn't want to put back on that wig which made my head so hot), I didn't want to leave that sweet precious time where I was being loved on.

≈

I came out of my experience with cancer a victor. I was not only victorious over that physical invasion in my body; I came out victorious over all the invasions of evil and the unfairness of life that had been perpetrated against me.

Some of the work that God was doing was a gradual process, but over time I began to change. I saw how many of the decisions I made in life were rooted and influenced by past hurts. I also came to see my parents' lives with new understanding. I realized my parents' lives were not anchored on Jesus, but their lives had rested on the stability of the religious establishment of the church. They started off with a strong moral compass and the expectations of the church gave them an outlined course to follow and principles to raise their children on, but they had no personal relationship with God. They did not surrender their lives to God. If they had declared so at one time, it was not always evident, because when crisis came and shook their foundation to the core, they fell apart. Apparently, their foundation was not the solid rock which is Christ.

I also came to the realization that apart from God, we human beings are really sinful and awful creatures. We can do atrocious things to one another. I don't excuse or rationalize my Wade's behavior towards me and I have never seen any evidence that the years had change him from the lurking python that I knew him to be. But as far as my response to him is concerned, I have been able to forgive him of the brutal ways in which he robbed me and other girls like me, of our childhood. God gave me a new heart towards my brother. He also gave me a love for Wade which had to be supernatural because there is no place on this earth where I could have gotten such a supply. Apart from his wife, I was the last family member to spend time with him before he died one fatal night at the young age of forty-two.

There are some people who were never meant for us even though we wanted them to love us in the worst way. I have come to realize that Romeo did not want me. He had affections for other people and other things even though he was married to me for thirteen years. He had left because he couldn't "find himself"; I didn't know what part of himself he had left with me, so I took multiple HIV tests to check that my body was not infected with the AIDS virus. I have also taken multiple doses of forgiveness lessons to come out clean and free from bitterness and resentment towards Romeo.

Today, as I reflect on this journey called my life, I think back to my beloved hula-hoop. I feel that no matter how well or expertly we can swing or maneuver the various things that life throws our way, we are just not as in control of our lives as we would like to believe. Sometimes the things we desire the most get away from us. Maybe it's a lover, a career, or a dream. We cannot control everything even though we may feel that we have a handle on things. We can blindly head off into some direction where a disaster or disappointment is waiting to blindside us, like that car that hit me head-on when I was running after my hula-hoop that fateful day. Fortunately, there is a God who has everything under control even when we don't. He alone can take life's tragedies and life's disappointments and use them to make our lives meaningful and worthwhile.

For me, He alone could have taken something so marred and make it whole. He alone could take my life which was so battered and bring healing to my deepest wounds. He alone could take my shattered life and put the broken pieces together in such a way to form something really beautiful.

Epilogue

The evening that I walked down the aisle to give my life over to Jesus was May 25th, 1993. It was a decision which changed my life and it also impacted the lives of many people since then. First, my father (whose life was a wreck) finally surrendered and gave over his life to Jesus in his later years. Jesus took away his desire for alcohol, healed his depressed spirit and turned him into man ablaze with passion for God. He died about a year after making that decision.

On January 6th, 2005, I got a super phone call from my brother Wendell. Wendell, who, for a while had taken a bad route in life, called me to say that he had turned his life over to Jesus. Since then he has become a changed man who is totally sold out for God. His family life is exemplary and admired by many people today. He is a serious soul-winner. It's not uncommon for him to go to church with twenty or more people following him each week. Recently Wendell told me that the dramatic change which Jesus had made in my life had a deep impact of him. It was my walk with Jesus that really inspired him to seek Jesus for himself.

My sister Ruby also said that ever since I started serving Jesus, both her and her husband desired to have the freedom, peace, and joy what they saw in my life. My brother-in- law Kevin would usually say that if Jesus gives me the amount of joy which he sees in me, it wouldn't hurt him to have Jesus himself. One day I took him up on his words and led him to the Lord. Both him and my sister Ruby gave their lives over to Jesus and they are dedicated Christians today. Ruby loves to share the gospel of Jesus Christ with other people. Kevin teaches Sunday school.

My brother Verdell Jr. died in a car accident April 16th 1995. The car was driven by a drunk driver. In the early hours of that day, he prayed with Wendell and gave his life over to Jesus. Little did he realize that he would be standing before Jesus within a matter of *hours*. If Verdell Jr. had not come to Jesus when he did, he would have spent the rest of eternity in Hell. I thank God that he came when Jesus called him.

Wade died July 21th 1991. His wife was left behind to tell a very interesting story. She told the rest of the family that two hours before Wade died, he was crying out to God. He was asking God to have mercy on him and to forgive him of his sins. Knowing how merciful God is, I believe that God forgave him of his sins and he is with Jesus today.

I continue to pray for my sister Sylvia, and my other family members. I pray that each will come into a real and personal relationship with Jesus.

My daughter, now grown with four children, has her own story to tell. Growing up in a dysfunctional home, she has been touched by many of the same bondages which I experienced in my family. Her experiences had left scars and wounds which God has lovingly healed. Her children and my grandchildren, now live lives that are free from the bondage of alcohol, molestations, and other such malwares of life. They have a grandmother and a mother who serve God and who sow positive seeds into their lives. They have blossomed into healthy and whole souls who are serving the Lord.

I lost touch with my childhood friend Kathy. After I got pregnant and ran away to North Carolina, Kathy also left Maryland and relocated to Okeechobee, Florida. I will always be grateful for that special friendship.

≈

I remarried in 1997 to a Christian friend whom I had known for 17 years. He is also a Lumbee Indian from Robeson County. Sam is someone who walks upright before God someone who is a true partner. Sam is my true love, my best friend, my gift from God. Sam and I continue to walk our last miles together preaching and teaching the word of God. Wherever God leads, we follow. We are enjoying our journey together serving the Lord. The Word of God says: "Can two walk together unless they agree?" (Amos 3:3). I am blest to be married to somebody who has the same vision in life as me. Sam reminds me of Jesus in the sense that he is gentle, humble, patient, and he doesn't like arguments and disputes. Sam is also very protective of me. Anyone who knows Sam knows that he is famous for saying, "If you disrespect my wife, you disrespect me." I never had a man who was keen on taking-up for me or making sure that no one offends or disrespects me before. I love him all the more for that.

Sam is a hard worker who provides for our home, plus he comes home each and every night like clockwork. His streak of calling me every day from his job just "to touch base" has not decreased for all the years that we have been married. Sam is the real thing. One just can't fake the real thing. Sam is also my number one supporter in ministry. He plays the guitar during worship, and oftentimes he plays softly while I am sharing God's Word. He sometimes jokes that he has his own Joyce Meyer. That's his way of saying that he is behind what God is doing in my life 100%. I love Sam and I thank God for blessing me with such a husband.

In addition to being Sam's wife, I am also a minister of the Gospel of Jesus Christ. My passion for the Lord really blossomed the year that I was diagnosed with breast cancer. It was during that time when I had spent so much time immersed in the Bible and in the presence of God, that I felt God was calling me to minister his Word. I ran for about five years, but one Sunday, I heard a message entitled "God is going to dig you up". The Holy Spirit let me know that He had dug me up from the depths in order to use me for His glory. I finally stopped running and said "God, here I am. Use me."

I started out teaching adult Sunday school classes in 2001. One great thing about teaching is that I learned more than anyone else during those years. I preached my first message at the pulpit on December 2, 2006. That experience reminds me of a woman in labor who gives birth for the first time. I experienced such real pain; my stomach was in knots and every nerve in my body was twisted up. It wasn't until I stood at the pulpit and started speaking that I experienced a relief and the supernatural blessing of God taking over and delivering His message through me. Hearing a message come forward out of my own mouth was as wondrous to me as seeing a new baby being born out of my womb. That first experience is something that I've relived many times. Today, I am still preaching and teaching God's Word. God has used me to change the lives of many people. God has used me to make a difference, he will use you too.

≈

I was the first one in my family to openly acknowledge that the one thing that was missing in my life was Jesus. I repented of my sinful ways and gave my life over to Him. Now most of my family members are saved. They are not just saved from eternity in hell, but they are saved from being slaves to such things like alcohol, depression, diseases which comes as byproducts of living without restraint, oppression, hopelessness, self-hatred, shame, guilt, contentious marriages and relationships, pornography, molestation, and lust.

You may be the only person in your family who's ever broken the barrier, the only one brave enough to stop doing what everyone else has been doing. What starts with you, can change a life and can possibly change a generation. Who knows how many others will change turn their life around because of the change they see you. On May 25th, 1993, when I took that first step towards Jesus, I never dreamed that today I would be where I am today. God will do the same for you too. Won't you take that step today?!

CPSIA information can be obtained at www.ICGtesting.com
Printed in the USA
BVOW08s2232110214

344633BV00001B/3/P